ANIMAL PASSIONS

FEATURING THE FINER FEELINGS OF THE FAMOUS FOR THEIR
FURRED, FINNED, AND FEATHERED
FRIENDS

EDITED BY
ALAN COREN

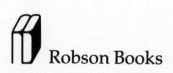

Robson Books

First published in Great Britain in 1994 by Robson
Books Ltd,
Bolsover House, 5-6 Clipstone Street, London W1P 7EB.
Compilation copyright © 1994 Alan Coren and CRC
Promotions Ltd

British Library Cataloguing in Publication Data
A catalogue record for this title is available from the British
Library

ISBN 0 86051 918 X

Typeset by Columns Design and Production Services Ltd,
Reading
Printed in Great Britain by Butler & Tanner, London and
Frome

Contents

O O O

David Attenborough	Gorilla Tactics	1
Barbara Cartland	My Dogs and I	5
Oliver Pritchett	Dawn Cacophony	9
Katharine Whitehorn	Gavin's Cats	13
Michael Palin	My Night With Betty	16
Clement Freud	Over the Styx	20
John Mortimer	Other People's Babies	23
Fay Weldon	Night Life of the Acre	26
Lynne Truss	And the Smile on the Face of the Dolphin	30
Frank Muir	Reigning Cats and Dogs	33
Valerie Grove	A Kind of Loving	36
Ian Hislop	Gregor Samsa's Revenge	40
Bob Monkhouse	What's Funny About Animals?	44
Paul Heiney	A Pig Like Alice	51
Libby Purves	Ram Raid	54
Richard Gordon	The Incredible Talking Dog	58
Tim Rice	How Now! A Singing Beast?	62

Barry Norman	I Know Two Things About the Horse	66
Keith Waterhouse	All Their Yesterday	70
Dannie Abse	Florida	73
Donald Trelford	Bushwhackers	76
Maureen Lipman	It Shouldn't Happen to a Pet	80
Christopher Matthew	Small Fry	84
Alan Plater	The Wild Pigs of Thorngumbald	88
Andrew Lloyd Webber	Semper Felix	92
Alan Coren	Sea Change	94
Ray Connolly	Black and White and Led All Over	99
Harry Secombe	The Dog That Wouldn't Lie Down	103
Michael Bywater	Outback of Beyond	107
Hunter Davies	Shellsuited	111
Matthew Parris	Dead Bats	114
Joan Bakewell	Beware of the Dog	117
Simon Hoggart	Citizen Coon	122
Alistair Sampson	Petty Points	126
John Wells	Monkeying Around	130
Leslie Thomas	Home Is the Hunter	135
Loyd Grossman	Subordinate Claws	139
Bel Mooney	Mrs Piggy	141
Frances Edmonds	The Bunny and Brush	146
Benny Green	Greyhound in the Slips	149
Claire Rayner	All Things Bright and, er . . .	156
George Melly	Cub Reporter	160
Dick Vosburgh	Doggerel for a Pedigreed Chum	163
Melvyn Bragg	Animals I Have Not Known	165
Gillian Reynolds	*Cage Aux Folles*	168
Michael Parkinson	Mitchum Rides Again	172
Roy Hattersley	The Donkey	176
Douglas Adams	Maggie and Trudie	181
Willie Rushton	Tailpiece	186

Editor's Note

o ◯ o

If you have ever wondered why a gathering of larks is called an exaltation, wonder no further: the larks gathered here raise the spirits like nothing else. But they raise more than that: all the royalties from this book have been donated by the writers to the Cancer Research Campaign, and while I thank my friends personally for all their delightful contributions, I thank them, too, on behalf of those for whom the word contribution means even more.

AC

David Attenborough

Gorilla Tactics

o O o

The opposable thumb. That, according to those who should know, is one of the key things a primate, on its way towards becoming human, has to have. With the ability to press thumb on forefinger, he or she has got a grip good enough to manipulate complex tools. From then on it is just a short jump to holding a pen, writing, tinkering with motor cars and other such accomplishments needed to create a civilisation. I was considering the matter because I was, some years ago, making a television series charting the history of life on earth. It was clear to me that I had to feature the opposable thumb. The question was, which non-human primate should we film to show it in action?

We decided on the gorilla. It was a somewhat ambitious choice for, at the time, gorillas had very seldom been filmed and hardly ever in situations where they were so relaxed as to be deploying their opposable thumbs with any degree of abandon. They were more frequently shown using them with the rest of their fists to thump their chests. There was only one chance. We heard that there was an astonishing American scientist, Dian Fossey, who had spent ten years with the gorillas in Rwanda and who was said to be able to sit alongside them almost as one of their family.

We wrote to Dian. To our huge delight and even greater amazement, she agreed to introduce us to her gorilla group.

The journey to Rwanda was not easy. There were strange and unpredictable African airlines, a perverse and wilful truck, and a very long tramp up the forested flanks of a volcano to Dian's camp. When we got there, Dian was seriously unwell. But, valiantly, she entertained us and instructed us in how to behave when approaching gorillas. You had to make burping noises as you approached to let them know you were around so that they could covertly inspect you. If they didn't like the look of you, they would make off and you would never get near them. If they didn't take offence, then you had to continue burping so they could continue to keep an ear cocked and check on just where you were. That was important because if you got very near without them knowing, they might be so startled they would charge. Standing upright or even lifting the head might be interpreted as a challenge. Better not. And don't talk loudly.

After several days of tramping around in torrential rains, and crawling, burping, through thickets of giant nettles and overgrown mountain celery, we at last got close to a gorilla family. Although we could not see them, we could hear them crashing about ahead. We were moving slowly and quietly down a hillside through very thick vegetation. Suddenly, we came into a clearing where the vegetation had been smashed flat. There on the other side sat an enormous female gorilla chewing celery. She looked at us coolly – and then went back to chewing. None of us had ever expected we would ever get so close and we were somewhat uncertain as to what to do next. We had already decided the previous night that the sequence was not to be about being intrepid or brave. Nor was it to be a mini-adventure story about how to get close to gorillas. We were making, after all, a scientific film. John, the director, was in charge. 'Just crawl as close as you can,' he whispered, 'then turn, and give us the stuff about the opposable thumb.' I didn't altogether like the sound of that. It would mean turning my back on the gorilla. I wondered if that was wise.

Martin, the cameraman, by now had his camera set up on a tripod. Dickie, the sound recordist, had finished pinning the radio mike inside my shirt. I crawled off.

To my surprise, the lady gorilla watched me with total equanimity. The closer I got, the bigger she seemed. She must have weighed, I reckoned, a good eighteen stone. With muscles to match. Perhaps it was my reluctance to turn my back on her that kept me going forward. At any rate, I eventually found myself within a yard of her. Very, very slowly, so as not to alarm her in any way, lying on my side, keeping my head low, and making a couple of burps just for safety's sake, I turned to camera. I was just about to start saying something when I felt a huge weight on my head. I twisted round. She had leaned over and put her hand on my head. In spite of the fact that, unquestionably, there was an enormous opposable thumb on my scalp, a little chat about it to camera did not seem appropriate.

With her hand still on my head, she lowered her own head and looked me steadily in the eyes. It would be untrue to say that her gaze was human-like. Her eyes were small, deep brown and without white around the iris. On the other hand I can truthfully say that I have never exchanged a look with an animal that seemed to have in it such understanding. Then she removed her hand and went back to chewing celery.

Perhaps this was the time to start my little talk. But then there was a tug at my foot. I looked down. Two infant gorillas, bundles of glossy black fur with sparkling bright eyes, were trying to undo my shoelaces. By now all thoughts of that thumb evaporated. I simply lay back to savour to the full the delight, indeed the ecstasy, of being accepted by these marvellous animals. There seemed no reason to be alarmed. Although I had crawled towards them, the last approach, the actual contact, had been initiated by them, not by me.

I'm not sure, even now, just how long I lay there. Eventually the infants scrambled off me and chased one another into the vegetation. The female heaved herself away for a couple of yards, just to keep an eye on them. I crawled back, feeling exhausted after having so much adrenalin pumping though my veins.

'I was quite alarmed at first,' said John. 'I thought she was going to twist your head right off – and the series is only half finished.' I took it that he was joking. 'But you didn't say anything about the opposable thumb,' he added. 'I was waiting for you to start and didn't like to cue the camera until you did.'

'You don't mean,' I said, 'that you didn't film anything at all?'

'Well,' he said, 'the other problem was that with her sitting beside you like that, people would think the whole thing was shot in a zoo. We've got to make it clear that we've been trekking about for days to get this. But in the end, she stayed so long that we thought we might as well shoot a few feet, just to amuse the cutting-room and the team back home.'

We met the gorillas several times more in the following days but we never got quite as close again and we never made physical contact with them. And I did, in less sensational circumstances, do my best to enthuse to camera about the opposable thumb.

The journey back was an eventful one. As we drove down the mountains in our truck, we were fired on by soldiers and eventually arrested. It seemed that some enemies of Dian's had spread a story that we were not making a film about gorillas at all but some kind of subversive documentary critical of the government. Standing, face to the wall, with arms in the air being body-searched, the danger uppermost in our minds was that someone was going to confiscate the gorilla footage and destroy it. Martin, when the first bullet whistled over his head, had taken immediate action. The crucial roll was already well concealed and he had decided what film we would sacrifice if a sacrifice was necessary. To our huge relief, it wasn't.

Eventually, we go the film back home. The cutting room was indeed amused, so much so, that even though it was not strictly relevant to our message, we decided to include some of the shots with the babies in the final film. And it could just be that people remember that, who have lost all recollection of the opposable thumb. As for me, I have to admit that it is not the first thing that comes into my mind when I think of that encounter in the Rwanda mountains. Which I do. Often.

Barbara Cartland

My Dogs and I

o O o

I have two wonderful dogs, one a white Pekinese called MaiMai
who replace Twi-Twi. He was the only living dog who has ever
been in Madame Tussaud's, and who also has a novel named
after him – *The Prince and the Pekinese*. Alas, when he was fifteen years old he went blind, so I had him put to sleep.

My other dog is Dickie, a beautiful black Labrador who
replaced Duke, of the same breed, which was given me by Lord
Mountbatten, the Christmas before he was assassinated, and
whose mother came from the Queen's kennels at Sandringham.

I am absolutely convinced the reason my dogs are so well is
that I have always given them vitamins. At the moment both are
having Selenium-Ace which I find not only a healer after any
small operation or infection, but also a prevention against cancer,
which unfortunately dogs have as well as human beings.

Actually one of my dogs, which had cancer of the throat, I had
put to sleep soon after I came to Camfield, and he has never left
us, but haunts the house, and we have all seen him many times.

I had Camfield Place blessed when I first came here and the

ghost dog came after the blessing, but no one is afraid of it as we know that he was so happy and loved us so much that he does not want to leave us.

One of the people I have admired so tremendously in the years in which I have kept animals, including cattle and a bull I loved very much, is Buster Lloyd-Jones, who I often spoke to when he was living a Hove. His son, Vernon Lloyd-Jones, owns a health shop and has the same interests and enthusiasm for vitamins as his father.

So many dogs, including Sir Winston Churchill's, owed their long life and health to Buster Lloyd-Jones. Now he is no longer with us, Denes have carried on his special foods like Healthmeal which is excellent for dogs, and his tablets of All in One Herbal Conditioner which I have found marvellous.

As it is a nuisance to try and persuade dogs to take tablets, I prefer to have them crushed up and put into their food.

I have found this is easy to do with Plus-Two tablets which come from Rayner and Pennycook, who have included in them, besides bonemeal, liver and seaweed, honey, which, as you know, I think is good for everyone.

For animals who are more amenable to taking extra supplements, Anima-Strath is the best tonic I can recommend for any dog or cat.

Like Bio-Strath, which I brought into this country many years ago and which has benefited millions of people all over Europe, Anima-Strath contains the cultivated yeast cells which are opened naturally by a fermentation process which I have seen taking place in Switzerland.

Old dogs, who have trouble with their legs, dogs who suffer from loss of hair, and those who lose their appetite and vitality are rejuvenated in an almost miraculous manner if they take Anima-Strath.

To get back to honey, not only is it a wonderful pre-digestive energy food, but it is also excellent for the heart and so many dogs suffer from some form of heart complaint without one being aware of it.

This is why I also include Vitamin E in the dogs' food, because there is nothing better than Vitamin E for the hearts of human beings.

What all animals need and which is very, very important, is the love that most people give them naturally, but some people forget they are like children and have to be continually reassured that they are wanted and that we care for them.

When I return from a journey abroad and see the two eager faces of my Labrador and Pekinese waiting for me in the hall, I know that their welcome is sincere and that they have not only missed me, but are thrilled that I have returned.

In fact, my Pekinese, from the moment he sees the boxes being packed, never leaves me for one moment, and when I first return home, invariably tries to sit as close as he can to me on my bed.

I always feel terribly sorry for animals in kennels who cannot know of the close and affectionate love we can give them in our homes, and I cannot bear to read reports of the dogs who are callously and cruelly let loose because their owners no longer want them and find them a nuisance.

The selfless love of an animal who has lived with us all his life is something which cannot be bought and is so precious that I think we are often not sufficiently grateful that we are the centre of their lives, and that being with them means contentment and a satisfaction that is greater than anything we can receive from another human being like ourselves.

We are their world, and this is something we must always remember when we take an animal into our homes and into our hearts.

An animal can never complain if other people are unkind to it when you are not there, an animal cannot tell you when he is upset, troubled, or even in pain. That is why it is extremely important that we watch them carefully, as we watch our beloved children.

I want to finish this article with a poem that I wrote to my Pekinese, Wong, who was with me for sixteen years of his life. He was proud, independent, obstinate, but loyal, loving and whole-heartedly mine. Could anyone ask more from a friend?

My Dog and I

For years you walked beside me every day,
    For years you slept upon my bed.
You showed your love in every way,
    I can't believe that you are dead.

If there's an after-life for me,
    Then I'd be lonely without you.
I must be sure that you will be
    With me, whatever I may do.

So I pray to God who made you and me,
    Who in death swept us apart,
To book a place in the 'Great To Be',
    For a dog with a loving heart.

OLIVER PRITCHETT

Dawn Cacophony

o ◯ o

It is fairly well known, I suppose, that I am one of this country's leading experts on birdsong. It takes concentration and a special sort of gift to be able to identify a bird just from a few notes of its song – particularly as birds do not usually go in for solos. They tend to favour choruses, starting well before dawn and continuing for the rest of the day.

I have trained my ear so that I can single out an individual bird from this jumble of noises and say, with some confidence: 'There is one of those large-ish brown ones somewhere among that lot.' Often, I can be more specific. I have learned, for example, that the song of one type of bird can sound exactly like a babble of all sorts of other birds. The call of a female grey serge sounds identical to the combined songs of four blue tits, nine starlings, thirty-two sparrows and a handful of thrushes.

A lot of this comes from experience. You soon learn that anything invisible overhead is a skylark. Or sometimes a Boeing. You can also be sure that any unnecessary outbreak of hysteria in the undergrowth is a blackbird's alarm call. Blackbirds are

9

extremely alarmist: the approach of even the most tactful ornithologist drives them frantic.

Another thing to remember is that a single type of bird may have a large repertoire. Sometimes people try to catch me out. They ask me what sort of bird is making that 'zik-zik-tseeta-tsee-ta' noise and I tell them it is a chaffinch. Then they say that a moment ago I told them that the bird going 'wim-nippy-ching-ching' was a chaffinch. Surely they cannot both be a chaffinch, they suggest.

I then have to explain to them that 'zik-zik-tseeta-tseeta' is the cry of a male chaffinch who has just landed on a dustbin. 'Hey,' he is crying. 'I've just landed on a dustbin.' On the other hand, 'wim-nippy-ching-ching' is the call of a female chaffinch warning off a common pipit that has strayed into her territory. 'Go away, you common pipit,' she is calling.

I have estimated that, at any one time, there are approximately 886,000 escaped budgerigars at large in the British Isles. No one has yet disputed this figure. It takes budgerigars only a couple of days to unlearn the snippets of human conversation they have picked up in captivity. This is important because some birds would have hysterics. So budgerigars now try to imitate the calls of large wild birds, like rooks and herons. If you find some bird-song that is difficult to identify it could well be a budgerigar having problems with its mimicry.

Meanwhile, ornithologists have recently revealed that urban birds are starting to imitate the sounds of their environment; they can make the noise of a car alarm or a fire engine or one of those chirruping telephones.

This is also true in the country. One type of collared dove, for example, has a cry which is just like a telephone 'engaged' signal. How this bird learned to make this noise is something of a mystery. My theory is that collared doves make their nests in remote rural telephone boxes (hidden away in those slots where telephone directories used to be kept) and that is where the young ones pick up the call.

Also, in the middle of the night in the country I often hear some bird give a strange plaintive cry of 'Byee!' then lots of others join in with the same 'Byeee!' I have never seen them, but they are obviously large birds – some sort of owl, perhaps – and I suppose they are engaging in some nocturnal mating display, because every so often they bang their wings against the sides of their bodies, making a noise that sounds uncannily like the slamming of a car door.

There are a good number of woodpeckers in my neighbourhood. People do not seem to realise that these birds often continue hammering away at the tree trunks well into the night. I have noticed that they have adopted a sort of disco-beat for their hammering.

We are lucky enough to have a nightingale in our garden. It sings throughout the night. There is nothing to beat that fabulous liquid sound of a nightingale – somewhat like a bathroom tap dripping.

Then, regularly at 5.30 in the morning, I am woken by the sound of a rare speckled redstart calling to its mate – that distinctive call which goes 'chink-chink-wheeze-chink'. The nearest equivalent noise, I suppose would be that of a milk float.

In the middle distance, when the wind is in the right direction I sometimes hear the joyful song of the yellow creeper. This shy little bird has learned to warn off larger predatory birds by imitating a 125cc motorbike.

Urban birds often migrate to the country. You may find a flock of starlings coming down on a Friday night, then suddenly taking off back to town on a Sunday evening. For a couple of days you can hear their exuberant fire-engine, car-alarm, ice-cream-van chimes and ringing-telephone songs.

Some of these birds, however, are clearly suffering from inner-city stress; their songs are much more shrill. Often the call of these birds is little more than a confused twitter because they are living on their nerves. There is a slightly violent edge to the urban privet warbler laying claim to his territory. A city-dwelling lesser crested tit has an unmistakable three-note call which sounds a bit like 'Give me strength!' while its country cousin has a smoother four-note cry which sound more like 'Never mind then'.

Experts have recently revealed that birds have regional 'accents'. In other words, a robin brought up in Yorkshire will sing a different tune from one brought up in the West Country. What may first sound like the mating call of a pie-eyed wagtail could easily be the cry of a speckled dunnock born in Dorset and blown off course by strong winds.

Birds also pick up foreign accents. Migratory birds can be affected by their experiences in foreign parts. A house martin or a swallow may be difficult to identify soon after its spring arrival in this country because it has acquired the song-patterns of birds around the water holes and plains of Africa. Even seagulls can be affected by a day trip to France, as they return with their harsh peremptory cries of 'Brie! Brie!'.

There is so much pleasure to be derived from listening to the birds. Everyone can recognise that particular rhythm of a wood pigeon's call, as it seems to be saying: 'I'm a hoopoe truly.' And that evocative sound of 'cuck-oo' drifting across the meadows in springtime is almost certainly our old friend the fugitive budgerigar, just practising.

KATHARINE WHITEHORN

Gavin's Cats

o O o

I married into cats. I didn't of course know what I was in for; I promised to love, honour and cherish and thought in my innocence that what I had promised to cherish was my husband, Gavin Lyall; not his blasted cats. For the first few months, everything seemed normal: we had jobs, we both got fired, we had rows, we both got repentant – the usual thing. Then we got cats. The only consolation is that it could have been worse: it could have been dogs. I don't think I could have stood all that drooling devotion: you remember Mike Leigh describing what happens if you're doing a bit of DIY? A dog will look at you and say 'I love you! I don't know what you're doing but it must be wonderful because I love you!' A cat will be thinking: 'I wouldn't do it that way if I were you.' A cat, at least, has some self-respect.

We applied, as did almost everyone else in North London at that time, to Georgie, who was then only on about her sixtieth kitten and had not yet reached the state where she would kick her kittens off the tit at four weeks to allow her to get back on the job, so the kittens were fairly normal in their behaviour. We called this first one Kilroy; and from that moment on a mysterious change took place in our relationship. Hitherto, when Gavin felt like stroking something, he stroked me. Not now; he stroked Kilroy. Until then, when we went to bed, it was just the two of us; now we had this animal snaking its way up my nightdress to get to Gavin. I loathed it; but they hadn't invented women's lib in those days and I was still at the stage of trying to be a Good Wife. So I put up with it.

Then Gavin decided (rightly, I have to say) that two cats are less trouble than one, so we got Sid. He wasn't called Sid at first, actually, he was called Algernon Aubrey St John Fishbreath, but couldn't live up to it. And Kilroy beat him up. All first cats beat up all second cats, as I now know; the only thing that varies is how long it goes on. In this case it took Kilroy two weeks to accept Sid, but us he never forgave. His malevolence manifested itself in glares, in tail-bristling fury and of course peeing pointedly in the wrong places; on one occasion he fixed Gavin with The Glare and started, but Gavin threw him across the room where he burst in a cloud of spray. Then he went missing, and stayed missing.

So then began the long procession of cats with whom I have shared my life ever since. Sindy, who could leap high in the air to catch a ball of paper, judging its trajectory so accurately that if it was going to fall in front of her she didn't move; Copper and Paddy and Singh (so called after Gavin had come back from India because he was black-haired and furious at all times); Flannel Foot and Susi and the dark Samantha with the bedroom eyes . . .

I became – I had to become – extremely good at getting rid of kittens. Innocent girls who came to deliver typing would find themselves going away with an appealing ball of fluff; friends suddenly became cat-lovers perforce; everyone in the office was assessed for their kitten potential within days of joining. The high-water mark of my kitten career must have been persuading Charlotte Bingham to take one, in spite of having two dogs, a rabbit, a horse and a child allergic to animals ('Why can't I tell the doctor about our animals, Mummy? He must be a very nasty man if he doesn't like animals'). That one, the product of an incestuous union with the mother's father, was ailing from the start; she nearly died, and was kept alive only by Charlotte leaving her in the middle of their double bed putting the fluence on her: 'You WILL survive' – and she lived to be twenty-two.

There was also the occasion when our helper, Trude, of Austrian extraction, persuaded a friend (ditto) to take one home after a party, using a small basket she usually used for carrying bottles; next day she complained bitterly when she couldn't find it, and had to be reminded . . . Gavin wrote the now kitten-owning friend a postcard, which said: '*Gemütlich*: German word hitherto thought untranslatable, but now understood to mean the ability of one Austrian, to accept a kitten which one of them does not own and the other does not want'.

We don't have kittens these days. We've put a stop to all that, now the children no longer need a lesson in the facts of life (and how). But an insidious change has come over my relationship with the cats: I think I'm beginning to become like them. We had one, Dolly, who would sometimes *rush* across the room, quick, to do something before she forgot what it was she wanted to do; I catch myself thundering upstairs for the same reason. And Martha, called after Martha Graham because of the grace with which she stretches – used to stretch – her back legs out behind her, is now, at fourteen, subject to nameless angst: she will sometimes stand and wail for a sadness she knows not what and some days I know how she feels. And the cat Sam is getting meatier and meatier, as she spends ever more of her time eating and takes less and less exercise . . . well, you can hardly expect a cat to do aerobics, can you? So why should I?

But they remain Gavin's cats, not mine, fond as I now am of them. It is quite good for my character, I suppose: to realise that though some may see me as wife, mother, columnist, or committee bossyboots, there are always two creatures around to whom I am simply a tin-opener with feet.

15

MICHAEL PALIN

My Night with Betty

o O o

We've lost all things in the car – money, cameras, virginity, boiled sweets – but very few of us can claim that our entire genital equipment has been jeopardised. It happened to me in a vintage 1936 Wolseley Hornet on a steep little road above the River Wharfe one balmy June night in 1984, and it was all Betty's fault.

I had first met her several weeks earlier. We were working on a film together. It was called *Pork Royale* at the time (it was later re-titled *A Private Function*) and Betty was the pork in question. She was a Sussex Ridgeback and had been literally born to play the part. There is not a great history of pigs in leading roles and her trainers felt that the process of domestication had to begin at birth if there was to be any chance of her performing the complex tasks described in Alan Bennett and Malcolm Mowbray's script. As soon as Betty could trot she was encouraged to climb up stairs, get into the back of estate cars, take fruit from bowls, stick her head in ovens, nuzzle trouser legs and all the hundred and one things that might come quite naturally to Zsa Zsa Gabor but require a massive evolutionary leap from a pig.

The first hint that nine months of concentrated conditioning might not have produced the perfect actress came on the first day of filming, in a sedate suburb of Ilkley, when it was revealed that there was not one but three Bettys – all, we were assured, interchangeable and equally talented. As it turned out one was too dangerous to allow on the set and the other never reached the set, being more interested in the local vegetation than the prospect of a BAFTA award. Betty the third had her own problems. Though she might walk quite confidently from her straw-bedded trailer to the front door, she became visibly, and understandably, agitated by the sight of a fully lit film set. The cry of 'Turn Over' and more particularly 'Action' produced an immediate result and Betty had to be led into the garden while the carpet was cleaned up.

Betty was especially partial to ginger biscuits and whilst an endless supply of these would keep her mind on the part it would also fill up her stomach creating a vicious metabolic circle until one day, quite suddenly, she went off ginger biscuits altogether. I remember Denholm Elliott shaking his head most thoughtfully at this. 'Quite amazing,' he muttered, staring down at her, ' . . . a Pauline conversion.'

Once off the biscuits Betty could be seduced only by sardine oil. This meant that any actor playing intimate scenes with her had to be smeared with the stuff. This was the reason why anyone taking a drive along by the River Wharfe on an early summer evening in 1984 might have seen two highly paid film technicians applying a fine coating of sardine oil to the handsome leather interior of a 1936 Wolsley Hornet. Some distance away they would have seen me having the same pungent mixture lightly applied to my trousers and the sleeves of my jacket.

It was quite a short scene. In it I was required to lure Betty down a grassy slope into the back of the car and then drive off. However, there was an edge of tension even before we'd begun. The film was running over-budget. Not by much, but enough to have the producers watching every move. The sequence was set at night, and night shooting is a producer's nightmare. The crew

17

is paid overtime until midnight, but go a fraction of a second beyond that and the whole business becomes a very expensive pumpkin indeed. The crew has to be paid an entire full day's wage. However, we were ready on time and Betty was summoned from her quarters and arrived at the top of the slope looking cracking. I thrust a well oiled trouser leg in her direction and off we went towards the car. Well, off I went. By the time I got to the car Betty was still at the top of the slope and showing no signs of sticking to the script. Almost overnight, the slope had sprouted into a field of wild garlic and the only thing that Betty evidently liked more than sardine oil was wild garlic. Try as we might to hurry and cajole her, the producers could only stand and bite their fingernails as Betty, pink skin glowing almost luminous under the great arc lamps, slowly and thoroughly ate her way down to the roadside. Once she'd ravaged the wild garlic she seemed to have little appetite left for the back seat of a Wolseley Hornet, even with its sardine-oil finish.

Betty's trainers were called up and the minutes ticked by as they deliberated. Eventually it was decided to double the coating of sardine oil and augment it with grain, pellets, cabbage stalks and anything else they could find in her dressing room. The camera rolled, Betty sniffed suspiciously. Finally she stuck her head and shoulders into the car and began to eat. But the heaviest part of my co-star was still sticking out into the road and a firmly-shut back door just bounded off her.

'Cut!' It was half-past eleven by now and Alan Bennett was beginning to chew the end of his tie. Presumably he saw the prospect of the whole scene being axed if it couldn't be completed within the half-hour. I felt for him, especially as the dour Yorkshireman who'd loaned us the car offered him some well meant advice: 'If I'd written this film, I wouldn't have put a pig in it.'

Then, quite suddenly and for no apparent reason, Betty heaved her massive bulk over the running board and onto the back seat. 'Action!' yelled the director, which I presumed meant me as Betty was well into action already. I slammed the back door and rushed round to the driving seat. When I got there I found to my amazement that Betty had clambered round and was sitting bolt

18

upright in the passenger seat looking out of the window – for all the world like an overweight housewife starting out on holiday. It was a brilliant piece of improvisation and, with a grin in her direction, I started the car and the pair of us drove out of shot. There were cries of laugher, joy and relief. It was five minutes to midnight.

The only person who wasn't celebrating was the cameraman. 'You got the shot didn't you?' asked the assistant director with a hint of desperation. Oh yes, he'd got the shot and very good it was too. In it was a pig, a car, an actor, and in the car window, as clear as day, the frozen reflected image of an assistant director. Alan reached for his tie and began munching. The pig trainers were yelled at to leave Betty where she was, the 1936 Wolseley Hornet was pushed back into position and I was raced into the front seat. 'Action!'

Betty could see no good reason why having turned in an Oscar-winning performance she should not be allowed back to the cab-bage stalks and wild garlic. As I started the car and let off the brake once again she made a wild lurch for the driving seat. I gasped, Betty snorted frantically and, evacuating most of the wild garlic and cabbage she'd already eaten, made to leap through the driver's window. It was like a Sumo wrestler trying to get out of an igloo. I yelled, Betty jammed, and down into my crutch was thrust a trotter with two hundred and fifty pounds of Sussex Ridgeback on top of it. A millisecond away from castra-tion, I released the wheel and grasped the descending trotter. The car veered wildly off into the lights, and skidded to a halt per-ilously close to a by now almost tie-less Alan Bennett. The door was wrenched open and I was pulled out leaving a vintage 1936 Wolseley Hornet full of pink quivering pig. Somewhere in the far distance, midnight struck.

CLEMENT FREUD

Over the Styx

o O o

As Nicholas James was jumping the third hurdle at Worcester last Wednesday, I turned to his trainer and said: 'When do we put him over fences?'

'Very soon,' said the trainer with a grin. Having pinged the first two, my gelding had jumped the next obstacle boldly, landed running, and gained two lengths on the mare who had been upsides at take-off.

This was the horse's first engagement over jumps. Last year, on his initial appearance at a racetrack, he had come a creditable fourth in a bumper at Ascot – proving that, apart from being a gentleman, exceptionally handsome and decently bred, he was also a racehorse.

He ran once more last year, in a two-mile National Hunt flat race at Sandown on going that was too firm: standing 17 hands, weighing around a ton, with big workmanlike feet, he needs give, and while the second run was disappointing, that previous race had provided a goodly number of winners and we retained optimism.

He summered in a field, got himself a leg, got warts, got better and two months ago, news filtered through that he was working well; then 'working better than horses who had demolished him on the gallops last year. He is good and ready to run a big race.'

As the rains came, we entered him lavishly; as the ground dried up, we took him out. Novice hurdles at Chepstow, Towcester and Wetherby all became slightly more valuable as the going firmed and Nicholas James's entry fees were forfeited.

At Worcester last Wednesday, having got rain over the weekend, the going was on the soft side of good. No more rain, but the professional view was that, while the going would be soft, the firm ground below should allow the horses to go through it. I spoke to my trainer in the morning. 'Bring your money,' he said.

I backed him at 12-1 before I left and brought some more money to reinforce the bet on the course.

It rained heavily most of the way up the M40. 'Pull him out and wait a week,' I said to myself; at Warwick, the rain stopped, the sun shone.

Samantha, who looks after Nick and led him around the parade ring, said he was extra well.

The horse looked wonderful, was nicely relaxed, but giving the odd twitch and shuffle to show that he knew it was an important occasion.

Richard Guest, who had ridden him at work, was in the saddle. I told him to come back safely and, as they left the ring to canter past the stands to the three-mile start, Hills laid me 16-1. This is a price that can be multiplied into round figures – like £5,000 to £300.

He settled nicely and, coming round the last bend before the home straight on the first circuit, he was in sixth place, which was exactly where the trainer had said he would like to see him.

Approaching the hurdle which would be the penultimate one next time round, he reached it, slipped on landing, crashed down and lay still. The jockey came off over his neck, got up. Nick lay there. The field galloped past.

After about 30 seconds, he tried to rise; lifted his head, used his front legs to push himself up like a performing seal, but the back legs would not co-operate. Down he went, a great, chestnut-coloured, heaving mound, and men came along with red flags to divert the field as they pulled my horse towards the inside rails.

I left the stands to walk to the penultimate obstacle . . . found it difficult to see exactly where I was going.

He tried to get up once more: raised his head, grappled with his front legs, collapsed. A dark green screen was put around him and, while I was still fifty yards away, I heard the shot. They tucked a canvas sheet under him, slid him up a ramp into the back of a van and I helped place the tarpaulin over his body.

My beautiful horse was dead, and with it my hopes for his future. When your friends die, you think back fondly at the good times you experienced. When a racehorse dies, at the beginning of his career, there is just an enormous emptiness as you mourn what might have been. Death has deprived you of your dreams.

Over the last two years, when something went wrong, it was all made better by the prospect of Nicholas James racing up the hill at Cheltenham, Nicholas James flying Beecher's. No more.

At airports they have chapels where some people pray for an uneventful flight and others give thanks for their safe arrival. I could have done with somewhere to sit quietly; racecourses do not make provisions for bereaved owners.

I would have liked to talk about the horse with my trainer, but he had a runner in the next: a runner whose owner had a right to expect a bright, optimistic man to welcome him into the parade ring. The show must go on.

I drove home after the fourth . . . and yes, I expect I will get over it, and no, not for a while, and possibly I will buy another horse. I shall not insure that one either.

Insurance companies ask you to put a price on the racehorse and I don't know how to value dreams.

JOHN MORTIMER

Other People's Babies

o O o

My grandmother had a particularly arrogant Pekinese named Ching. He had a squashed face and the expression of a Manchu emperor ordering an instant decapitation. On the whole Ching was a lazy dog who, if taken for walks, looked as though he expected to be carried on a litter. When, threading his way disdainfully along some woodland path, a few leaves or a small twig became attached to his behind, he would stop dead in his tracks until a human lackey had removed this insult to his dignity. My aged grandmother would play at bullfights with Ching. She would caper about her resinous, pine-planted garden in Surrey flapping his blanket at him, performing a double *passada* as Ching charged at her, yapping wildly, whilst Granny 'was great in there with the cape all the long, hot afternoon'. One evening, when I was extremely young, I was crawling on Granny's hearthrug, pretending that I was a diver in the depths of the ocean: I saw a mighty whale and swam towards it. The whale turned out to be Ching, who bit me quite savagely on the cheek. Since then I have learned to be wary of other people's pets, as I am of other people's children.

Other people have cats and many, including one of my greatest friends and my television producer, love these animals. I can't stand them. They are meant to be aloof and proud and quite above caring for the love and affection of the inferior human race. I only wish that they would behave in this admirable manner when I come to call. No sooner have you sat down in a cat-infested house when some bloated portion of the hearthrug leaps onto your lap, unsheathes its claws and tramps about in search of a comfortable lie-down. In no time at all the trousers are penetrated, threads tear and finally a heavy and mouse-filled weight flops down on your genitalia. On the whole this animal is about as aloof as a drink-crazed sex offender.

The trouble with other people's pets is that they do tend to home into the crutch. Open the front door of the keeper of long-haired terriers and, with a fusillade of barks, a number of furry exocets hurl themselves at your flies. Sit at dinner with a family devoted to lurchers and, as you pick at your parmesan, quails' eggs and rocket salad, you will feel a warm and eager intruder between your thighs which, to your embarrassment, or perhaps disappointment, turns out not to be your hostess. Any sudden reaction, such as a swift kick or striking the animal with the desert spoon, will be looked upon by your hosts with disapproval; but there is really no polite way of getting a lurcher's nose out from under you. Other people's pets can give rise to even more embarrassment. I remember, long ago, a cameraman who insisted on bringing his pet gibbon to the set. It was then that we learned that it's impossible to house-train a monkey.

My father and mother weren't great ones for domestic animals but I first went into the pet business with a couple of white mice named Cyril and Maud after an actor-manager, famous in my father's day, named Cyril Maud. At first, like Adam and Eve in the Garden of Eden, they were alone, but they began to emulate that early couple by producing an entire race. Soon we were buying more and more cages, equipped with little treadmills for the creatures to play on; and the garage became the home for innumerable Cyrils and countless Mauds. I can remember the awful smell of them to this day, and the bottoms of their cages, a beige and black mixture of mouse-droppings and sawdust, which looked just like some of the more expensive breakfast cereals.

My first wife, when I first knew her, had an untrained dog christened 'dog', who lived on herrings in tomato sauce eaten from the tin and, for exercise, would run behind her car. Only in a second marriage did I discover someone able to cope with pets. I have become ridiculously fond of the dogs we have looked after and this particularly applies to the first of these few. Jackson was a white mongrel. I don't know what he had in him, bits of bull-terrier, collie, spaniel perhaps; anyway the effect was handsome. He was good-natured and became so friendly that I could walk across the Strand from my chambers in the Temple and he would trot beside me without a lead. He used to come to 'Rumpole' rehearsals (I remember Leo McKern accusing him of being too thin) and, on visits to my accountant, he would slink under the table and lie there in an attitude of total depression. Sitting by the fire in our living room he could sense the intrusion of a deer into the far end of the garden; this would cause him to stand up and quiver slightly. One night, when I was alone with him in the house, he stood up quivering at some distant excitement. He had a curious look in his eyes and his whiteness seemed unearthly. I opened the French windows, he shot out and I never saw him again. Later we heard of a white dog being shot for chasing sheep.

Now we have a charming, almost obedient, Labrador and a totally unbiddable, anarchic and ferociously intelligent Jack Russell. Their favourite pastime is barking at people extremely loudly. They can sense the milkman when he is half a mile away, travelling through the darkness before dawn. They will then bay ferociously and awaken far distant neighbours. The postman won't come through the gates because of them, but he keeps his pockets full of biscuits which he throws to them. They gobble the biscuits but bark even louder. The postman is right. You can never trust other people's pets.

FAY WELDON

Night Life of the Acre

o O o

From the air, Las Vegas seems the most brilliant and vigorous of all the night cities: and by that token alone the most villainous, sucking up as it does and spewing out into the desert air, by the multigigowatt, the stored resources of the world's past: twisting the arm of the helpless jungles and forests of the Pliocene Age, long ago compacted into oils and gases, to serve the riotous passions and pleasure of the present. The extortion racket to end all extortion rackets. The night air of Vegas quivers, if you ask us down here in Somerset where a passing aircraft wouldn't even notice our existence, not just with electricity but with ecological sin. Forget the girls, the gambling, the Syndicate: forget sex if you can, *what about the planet?*

But then we would say that, wouldn't we? We are so used to defending the moral high ground here in rural England. Indeed, we slumber at our posts and could say it in our sleep. I only mention Vegas because sometimes, when I grope for the switch of the 40-watt bulb which dimly lights the garden path so that guests can evade our dogs, or shift the angle of the solar power lamp –

given a clear day it sucks up sunlight and returns it, albeit grudgingly, by night – the better to deter the fox from the goose-house,
I find myself wishing that I were there, not here. I wish I were
wearing four-inch heels and feeding coins into some state-of-the-
art fruit machine, one which pinged its pleasure at every success
and sang Congratulations, Jubilations in a tinny voice as the
wheels span.

Here, in the acre, abroad at night, you sometimes hear the sudden beat of the barn owl's wings, and stomp home through the
mud to tell. It is so silent. Money has to be worked for, not won.
Insanity.

Don't think for one moment that because it's dark and quiet,
and there are no street lamps and only the Milky Way to reassure
you the sky's not falling in, that it's peaceful here in the heart of
the country. It isn't. You can't fall on the bed drunk or high, as
you can in the city, and just pass out for the night. No. First you
have to shut up the hens, the geese and the ducks in their separate houses, decipher the cat's wishes either to go out or stay in
the house all night: pound up wire wool and chilli powder to bar
the rat's entry.

Or you have to sit up all night for your own particular fox or
the neighbourhood rogue badger, who in one week, they say,
killed seventy hens, and snapped the locks on six hen-house
doors, and broke down four others altogether. If it was a badger,
and not the devil himself, who round these parts takes the shape
of a giant black cat, who comes out of the night, and stares in
windows, and looks, and passes by.

And don't think shutting animals away for the night is simple,
either. They're temperamental. They sulk, They're suicidal. The
ducks and the geese take time to argue nightly as to whose house
is whose, while night falls and the fox prepares to pounce. Hiss,
quack and flurry. The hens will go in at the first hint of chill in
the air – not the others. They like to cut it fine. *Why* foxes decide
to attack only after lighting-up time defeats me. Sometimes, of
course, they don't, and do. Then you are indeed defeated, and
there's blood and feathers everywhere. But on the whole, all animals keep to their unspoken rules: as if there were some agreed
Geneva Convention as to who was legitimately allowed to eat

whom and when and under what circumstances. Nuts!

As to this argument about duck house or goose house, the geese, large, excitable, powerful birds, believe they live by right in the duck house. But it's too small. Once the littlest goose, cramped for space, broke a wing in some midnight mêlée; and if too confined they'll trample their own eggs to bits, into a disgusting sludge of yolk and shell, hay and slime. It's just that they like the duck house: and custom and practice and fury keep them dodging out of line as you drive them in what they think is the wrong direction, and diving with their huge beaks at your ankles, and you can feel the fox out there somewhere in the hedge, watching and jeering.

And the ducks, likewise, love the goose house and, led by the Indian Runner, a scuttling bird with a long neck which always looks as if it's going to fall flat on its face, and is far too fast for its waddling devotees, every evening make their own bid to pre-empt it; which they do by charging in, falling instantly asleep and refusing to wake.

And what was that midnight mêlée, anyway? The noise of it woke us up. Perhaps the big devil cat with its slit-yellow eyes peered in through the wire mesh, and in the morning the littlest goose had to have its wing splinted.

Life in the hen house isn't all roses, either. We have two cockerels to eight hens. Cocks will fight to the death, and the victor lay his claw upon the torn and bloody vanquished and crow his triumph to the world, while the silly hens crowd round, in admiration and adoration. But our two seemed just fine together. Until one day the smaller one took on the large. The smaller creature won, being wily: the large, old, stupid bird surrendered, survived, recovered, but now, despised by all except one faithful fluffy-legged bantam, eats second to last. The one who eats last is the bantam, who thus saves him from complete humiliation. She scuttles in late at night too, to crouch in the corner with her disgraced beloved: neither are allowed up on the perch. A cruel place, this acre. Not just the fox to fear but the censure of the species.

The fox, making an untimely raid, did indeed one day get the gander as he squabbled with the ducks. Told you so! The littlest goose then refused to go home at all but spent a week of nights down in the reeds by the pond, grieving. The fox left her alone, as some Mafia boss might leave the moll of an executed gangster as a public exercise of power or a declaration of charity, or both. Presently she wandered home and fell in love with a sister goose. They're inseparable. Perhaps it's a gentler relationship, who's to say, than the one she had with the gander. She was the one who had her wing broken in the mêlée. What *was* it about? I suppose we'll never know.

We never eat these birds. It would feel like cannibalism. Goose eggs work out, I suppose, at about £5 each; duck eggs, if you can find them, at £3. Hen eggs 75p each. But at least you know where they've been – as if that thought wasn't disgusting enough. Sometimes I think the world would be a better place, or at any rate fairer, if instead of boys having mothers of the delightful opposite sex, and girls having to put up with mothers of the same boring sex, both genders could crack ourselves open out of eggs. Every home with its own nesting box, under the stairs? Ideas like this don't come in Vegas: only in Somerset when you raise the goose crook high: Director of the Universe! Las Vegas, I forgive you your sins, bright city of the wasteful night. I wish I were there, not here.

LYNNE TRUSS

And the Smile on the Face of the Dolphin

○ ◯ ○

So there we were on an open boat, half a mile out from Amble Harbour in Northumbria, choppy and wet but not downhearted, when a South African women finally asked the question that was niggling all our minds. 'Dr Dobbs,' she said, drawing tight the rubber strap of a snorkel-mask and zipping the neoprene wetsuit up her middle, 'why does Freddie the friendly dolphin always have his penis erect when he swims with us?' Horace Dobbs smiled knowingly into the sharp wind; he was an expert on dolphins, especially Freddie. 'The dolphin is the only animal in creation that can control the erection of its penis by will,' he explained, proudly. 'So the answer is, Freddie trusts us. Don't forget, he is a large wild animal yet he chooses human company. This penis thing, you just mustn't be anthropomorphic about it.'

I remember how we all smiled weakly and said 'Oh' and 'Right', unconvinced. Anthropomorphism notwithstanding, the South African woman was extremely attractive (wet T-shirt and everything) and within half a minute of her splash into the cold murky North Sea, friendly Freddie had hooked her with his penis and was dragging her away from the boat to a nice little place he knew. If this was trust in action, it was taking forms Johnny Morris wouldn't know about, and would clearly involve the swapping of telephone numbers before he'd let her go. As if all this weren't conclusive enough, a chap from Hull later replaced the exhausted South African in the water and tried to cadge a similar ride. Freddie bit his hand, thrashed about a bit, and then dodged off harbourwards for a spot of lunch.

Why was I aboard this open boat? For two reasons. First, because I had heard Dr Dobbs's persuasive theory that swimming with dolphins is a corrective to depression, and I thought it might make an amusing piece. And second, because the idea of lone dolphins living in cold British harbours gave me a quasi-religious thrill, adjacent to awe. Dolphins are not only beautiful, but are considered to be cleverer than a bucketful of brains, and I like to think they confer their presence on harbours like a blessing. Not everyone agrees with this starry-eyed view, I know. At Dingle in Ireland, swimmers who have spent long patient years getting friendly with Funghi the dolphin have noticed with regret that Funghi's superintelligence will not prevent him suddenly abandoning their mental inter-species symposium to dart off and play with a rubber glove. Unimpressed Dingle residents sometimes pooh-pooh Funghi's attention to humans, pointing out that actually cows take as much notice of people in a field. 'Next door's budgie recognises the sound of their sister's car,' said one.

But as for Freddie, I was in love with love and wouldn't listen, even though reason should have told me I had now placed myself in a situation for which I was profoundly ill-equipped. Back on the boat, having fastened a borrowed wetsuit (in an unpleasant shade of grey pork sausage), tied my straggling hair and strapped a painfully nose-squashing snorkel to my face, I dithered on the edge and had qualms. The trouble was, I had not been out of my depth in water before. I could swim a bit, but only in three-foot shallow pools designed for toddlers and baptisms. I looked down and my lip quivered. This dirty radioactive deep deep sea offered drowning possibilities beyond my wildest nightmares. And while dolphins in classical literature were occasionally known to save human lives, it's obviously an unwise person who would count on it.

So I took off the mask and said I'd better not. The others groaned. Kindly, Dr Dobbs said I could cling to a lifebelt and peer through the hole in the middle at the friendly dolphin, while he dragged me into position, which seemed like a good plan, except that I just couldn't imagine getting into this horrible water without first being bagged by a tranquillizer gun. I dithered, and they groaned again. So finally, because the others were beginning to complain of the cold and because there was no opportunity to make a break for it, jump in a car and drive off – I went down a ladder into the water, and let go. Only readers who scream (like me) while watching Jacques Cousteau on television can properly appreciate the enormous courage this last bit required.

I have a photograph of my encounter with Freddie the dolphin. Someone on the boat sent it to me, and I have to say it doesn't look like the scene of a great adventure. You can see Dr Dobbs in a smart red hooded wetsuit pulling the lifebelt, and then me horizontal and grey like a bloated corpse with my face earnestly in the water, listening to my own heavy breathing amplified by the snorkel, and gripping so hard on the rubber ring that my arms hurt for a week. And in the foreground of the picture, about twenty feet from our little group, you can see Freddie the friendly dolphin swimming eagerly towards the boat away from me, as if to say, 'Where's that brunette with the T-shirt? Is she coming in again?'

Rejected even by a dolphin who can control its penis by conscious will, it's the story of my life. But it still cheered me up considerably, this 'swim' with Freddie in the North Sea. I felt so fantastic that I wrote a gush of unusable New Age twaddle for the *Independent on Sunday*. Later, when Freddie became the focus of a dolphin sex-abuse scandal (the chap was acquitted), I felt I had knowledge relevant to the case, but I was never called to bear witness, which was a shame. I wanted to explain that the lone dolphin not only inhabits a frictionless world teased by glimpses of nubile South Africans in rubberised outfits, but has tragically evolved without arms. But it would have been in poor taste, I expect, so I didn't.

FRANK MUIR

Reigning Cats and Dogs

o ◯ o

I mean, I've got nothing personal against the five assorted animals who live the life of Riley in our midst. Three cats and two dogs. Furry denizens of the furniture all day, when they're not tearing bits off it. And eating. Oh, my goodness, eating; tin after tin of the gourmet stuff as advertised and refusing even to look at commoner nourishment. Never mind. Only the best is good enough for our silent dependants. And then there are things like their flea-collars at about three quid each (most of my mind was on higher things when I first saw the notice 'Flea-collars' in the pet-shop window – I found myself idly wondering how one buckled it round the neck of such a small insect . . .). But no begrudgement. Health before wealth.

It's just that, well, perhaps we should not allow ourselves to get too soppy over our pets. There is another side to them which, as we have no memory of pain, we tend to forget. Perhaps we should reconsider this not-so-attractive side of domestic animals, if only to remind ourselves that animals, however loveable, are only pets, while we are – well, us.

The French poet Méry once rather impressively declared (and in French, too) that a cat was God's way of allowing man to caress a tiger. A piece of sentimental twaddle, I humbly submit, only to be expected from a nineteenth-century Frenchman with a Christian name like a pop group of three garçons and a fille – François-Joseph-Pierre-Agnes. I have never, myself, personally, caressed a tiger – my arm is about twenty feet too short – but years ago at the London Zoo I once caressed a cheetah, a similar make of beast, and I can report that caressing a cheetah is like stroking a wire flue-brush. It can draw blood.

Blood is never far from the surface with cat owners. Our three cats, two Burmese and an Abyssinian, sleep in the bed with us. They have decided so to do and it is impossible to keep them out, so no moral or hygienic judgements, please; let us just say that at least they keep the foxes down. In the middle of the night cats need to stretch, so they stretch, at the same time unsheathing their little scimitars and swiping out at the nearest soft surface. I caught sight of my back recently in the bathroom mirror and I look like a steel engraving from *Foxe's Book of Martyrs*.

It is my belief that your average mog is a mass of finely tuned instincts and sophisticated reflexes but in the matter of intelligence is as thick as a Sumo wrestler's thigh. What sort of mighty hunter can't locate its food even when you've rammed its nose into the saucer?

When there is a bit of cold chicken left over in the fridge it becomes the sole objective of our three cats to get at it. Nestles (the greediest) is the stakeout man. He sits three feet away from the fridge door, *willing* it to swing open. He will wait there for days if necessary. Cinto, the Abyssinian, is an outdoor lad so he occasionally livens up Nestles's lonely vigil by dropping in and showing him bits of an ex-mouse. Gentle, middle-aged Kettering is the peter-man. Once they have decided in their minuscule brains that the remains of the cold chicken carcass is not going to leap out and surrender, nor the fridge door melt, Kettering starts work on the bottom edge of the door with a gently probing claw. The fridge is often improperly closed due to something like a £1.08 litre-bottle of Turkish Chablis keeping the door slightly ajar, and Ketters often *can* open it. But then what happens? The three Great Thinkers tip the cold chick on to the floor and then haven't the faintest idea what to do with it. It is suddenly too big, or something. It looms over them, cold, alien, and the wrong colour, nothing like *real* food, like their beloved chunks of shiny, brown meat out of a familiar tin marked 'Carlton Pet Foods: 38p'. So they affect indifference to the mess on the floor, yawn, blink slowly several times and stroll off.

The dogs, too, have IQs difficult to discern with the naked eye. Our scrap of black mongrel, Battersea, named after the Dog's Home whence we sprang her, is an ingratiator. Visitors get an all-over lick, and a liquid look which says: 'Take little me home with you; I am so badly looked-after here.' This is true. We don't even clean her ears out for her. We take her to the vet now; he's a sixteen-stone New Zealander and can just hold her down if she's under a general anaesthetic (£33.50).

And as for our pedigree standard poodle, Bognor Regis: aristocratic beauty . . . 10/10 marks. Sense of fun . . . 10/10. Affectionate nature . . . 10/10. Canine instincts . . . 10/10. Brains . . . well, look at it this way. As I type these critical comments, Boggy is lying down under the desk keeping me company, as is her wont. She knows that I am saying nasty things about her and the other animals because I read aloud as I work. But will she do anything about it? Will she get her own back on me in some way? No, because that sort of thinking would require an understanding of cause and effect of which she, as a dog, is quite incapable.

No, she will just lie there on the carpet and continue playing innocently with the cable of my electric typewriter.

Now she has started giving the cable playful little bites, but I don't mind: to the world she may be an inferior creature of little intelligence, but I will always think of her as my friend.

VALERIE GROVE

A Kind of Loving

o O o

Men love women, women love children, children love hamsters – the hopeless human triangle was summarised by Alice Thomas Ellis. As you must have noticed, children generally prefer pets to parents, a fact nowhere better illustrated than in Nicola Beauman's biography of Cynthia Asquith. When Cynthia was a child, her pet dog, Paddy, died. They told her as gently as they could, and to their surprise she just carried on playing with her toys. So later, they were even more surprised when Cynthia asked, 'Where's Paddy?' 'But we told you,' they said. 'Paddy's died. You didn't seem to mind very much.' At which she broke into howls of tears, saying, 'I thought you said "Daddy"!'

Inside my own mature exterior is the erstwhile child who cried for a week, at age ten, over a mawkish American book called A *Letter to the Man Who Killed My Dog* about a run-over beagle. Even later, there was a time when I was besotted by my cat, Jeremy. Every year on his birthday, 8 November, he would have a party, with a salmon-flavoured cake and champagne, and grownup guests singing as he blew out his candles. How babyish

36

can you get? Then one cold winter morning he walked out and was never seen again. I was inconsolable. At pushing thirty! I shed buckets of tears: put notices on trees, offered rewards, scoured the mean streets of Kentish Town. At the time, I was hugely pregnant with my first baby. She was born a month after the disappearance of Jeremy. So I can date very precisely when my soppiness over animals came to an abrupt and final end. After the child, and subsequent children, all animals became no more affecting than any other furry toy. We have had several cats since then – one an absolute ringer for Jeremy and named Jeremy II. At least two of them have vanished or been run over without a single tear being shed by me. My only involvement with The Cat in our house – decorative but vicious, depositor of half-eaten mice and wood pigeons on bedroom carpets – is as addressee of letters from the increasingly grand vet, reminding me that Smokey Grove is due for a booster dose, an injection against cat flu, or to have his spiky little teeth cleaned. The bill is never lower than £80.

The children, of course, are all as soppy as I once was, shrieking and drooling every time the cat stretches or pounces or goes about his feline business. They remind me of Noël Coward and his response to Beverley Nichols when he arrived at Nichols's house and was asked whether he minded cats. 'Dear boy,' said Noël, 'my fondness for all animals is such that I cannot see a water-bison without bursting into tears.'

Ah yes, I too once got shivers down the spine when *Pony* magazine dropped on the doormat; learnt by heart 'The Donkey' and D H Lawrence's 'Snake' with its affecting line, 'And I wished he would come back, my snake'. My sister and I had a special dog-language in which to communicate with our Staffordshire bull-terrier Sable –yuk! In hard-hearted mid-life, I am convinced that being besotted by animals is infantile; in ageing married couples it almost invariably signifies indulgent infant-substitution, when children have flown: they cannot live in a flat, leave England, stay in a hotel, 'because of Mitzi' or whoever occupies the best armchair.

I now prefer animals on the page, preferably when they display a robust contempt for humankind: like Saki's Tobermory, or

37

Thurber's grumpy Airedale Muggs, The Dog That Bit People: 'My mother said he was always sorry after he bit someone . . . but I don't know. He didn't act sorry.' I like Tramp in *The Lady and the Tramp*. I like Chumley, the chimpanzee that rode in the sidecar of Gerald Durrell's motorbike, smoking a cigarette, and grabbing at astonished cyclists; and Rose Macaulay's ape in *The Towers of Trebizond* that took a solo joy-ride in a Morris Minor; and the monkey that snatched Oliver Cromwell from his cradle and sprinted up to the rooftop with the infant Protector in its prehensile grasp; I love Dominick Dunne's description of Enid, Lady Kenmare, who 'would make her entrance with a parrot on one shoulder and her hyrax – a small ungulate mammal with the incisors of a rodent – on the other.'

There is always something especially crazy about ladies who go about in society challengingly draped with live fur: fashion editors are especially prone to this. Lucy Lambton is as enraptured over dogs as she is about lavatories, sinking to her knees awash with goodwill at the mere sight of a wagging tail. She is frequently to be found prostrate on a chaise-longue, cradling some sickly dachshund, and she has a memorial to her past dogs in the hall, inscribed 'Joyfully Barking in the Heavenly Chorus'.

P G Wodehouse summarised the syndrome: he wrote to his friend Bill Townend, didn't he agree that as one went through life all one needed was a few good friends, a wife, a swimming-pool and a Peke? The appeal of Pekes eludes me . . . but wait. Even as I write I begin to sense incipient infantile zoophilia returning *chez nous*. The eldest child will soon leave home. Even the youngest is now hard-hearted enough to stride off up to the hillside with a .22 rifle, return holding a dead bunny by its heels, and watch it being skinned, disembowelled and boiled for supper. But the boy is eleven, just the age at which any aspiring William needs a Jumble trotting at his heels. And I ask, when children outgrow parents, towering above us with great elongated limbs and size ten Doc Martens, who can you pick up and hug?

Last Christmas, I bought a charming lifesize plaster Dalmatian for my husband. He sits, benignly smiling just like Gus, the Dalmatian we once owned, by the fireside. A good way of owning a dog without tins of smelly Chum, walking, moulting etc, I thought. But every time I see him sitting there so obediently, I feel this mid-life crisis coming on: dear Gus, so handsome, so cheeringly companionable, how have we managed without you? And after all, what hearth is complete without a dog?

Ian Hislop

Gregor Samsa's Revenge

o O o

I have no doubt that somewhere in this country there is a charity devoted to the welfare of cockroaches. It is even quite likely that it has a militant wing who go round in balaclavas attempting to stop people treading on them. This article will unfortunately place me on their hitlist since I have to admit that I have deeply unsound views on cockroaches. In fact, as far as cockroaches go, my opinions are well to the right of the *Daily Mail*. Capital punishment is the only possible solution, and indeed hanging is far too good for them. A solid whack with a shoe is the only language they understand. My hard-earned reputation as a liberal will just have to take second place in this debate to my obsessive and undying hatred for cockroaches.

As any therapist will tell you, if you pay them enough money, this sort of deeply held resentment is always the result of some form of trauma involving the object of the neurosis. And it is true in my case. My loathing of this orthopterous insect dates back to an incident in India which I can only describe as The Night of the Living Roach. Like all horror films it began with a young couple looking anxiously for somewhere to spend the night as the sky began to darken. I was that young couple. Well, I was half of it, anyway, and I was the half clutching a copy of *The Lonely Planet Guide to India* which had brought us to Cochin in Kerala. This province on the south-west coast of the sub-continent was notable at the time for having the only democratically elected communist local government in the world. To be honest it was not this, though, that had drawn us there, fascinating as a comparative study of the amenities of, say, Lambeth Council and the Keralan equivalent would have been. The real reason for our visit had been to see the lush tropical forest, the coastal lagoons, the old port of Cochin with its bizarre Indian Jewish quarter, the ancient Chinese fishing nets which the locals still use, and the dancers who perform the traditional mime of Kathakali. (You'll have noticed that I've still got the guidebook.)

Anyway, we had managed to pack in most of this during the day (including two hours of mind-numbing Kathakali which makes Morris dancing seem like an under-rated art form) but we needed to find a bed. The fact that it was bucketing with rain added to our urgency and we headed for the Bolgatty Palace, a converted eighteenth-century Dutch palace on an island which you had to reach by boat. It was deserted, since most travellers, unlike ourselves, had not chosen to visit Kerala during the monsoon. The receptionist eventually told us that contrary to appearances they had no rooms available in the main hotel but that we could have a 'honeymoon cottage' in the grounds. These were small, squat, brown structures which were apparently very popular with newly-weds. We did not fit this category but we were very wet and tired and felt that we did not have much of a choice.

It was then that I saw the first cockroach. He was sitting on the stair near the reception and almost blended in with the old carpet. He is really quite large, I thought to myself. I was not an expert on the species but we had seen a few of them in the drier parts of India and they had looked an awful lot smaller than him. However I said nothing, thinking that there was no point in overreacting to the presence of a salutary if sizeable roach minding his own business a few feet away from me. Besides we were not staying in the old wooden palace anyway but in a new modern cottage in the grounds.

A cheerful boy led us out to our 'romantic accommodation' holding a large golf umbrella over our heads as the rain had decided to turn into a torrential flood. The boy opened the door to the building, turned on a very dim light bulb, and then left us.

There was only one room, which was entirely circular. It had brown walls and a brown floor. In the middle of the room was a brown circular bed. There was a window covered by brown curtains. My wife stood by the bed and looked rather conspicuous in a white jacket. Except that it was not all white. There was a large brown patch on it which was moving towards her head.

This time I could not ignore the cockroach and leapt into action managing to get it onto the floor and under my foot with only a small amount of screaming. Mostly from me. Having killed it, I decided that I would draw a line under the incident by throwing its remains out of the window. This was a mistake as the action of drawing the curtain aside disturbed a large number of cockroaches who had previously been camouflaged against the brown material and who began to run up and down the curtain furiously. One of them went across my hand and another ran down the brown wall heading towards our bags. Another one scuttled onto the brown floor and underneath the bed. Something in me snapped and I gave a poor though frenzied impersonation of the Terminator, dispatching huge numbers of cockroaches Schwarzenegger-style with only a lightweight shoe as a hand-weapon. The body-count was horrendous. But still they kept coming.

Eventually a sort of exhausted truce was reached and I think they agreed to stay out of sight if I agreed to put my shoe back on. My wife and I then sat fully clothed in the centre of the circular bed with our bags beside us taking it in turns to stay awake and keep guard. For a couple of hours we managed sentry duty like this, listening to the pouring rain and straining in the gloom to spot the ominous brown shapes moving against the brown decor. Then during my third watch came the last straw. I had noticed that where the builders had installed the central heating there was a large hole leading straight outside. As I gazed round the room checking for signs of roach activity I always ended looking at this hole. And my vigilance was rewarded. After a flash of lightning and a roll of thunder an intruder burst right through the hole and into the room. That's a very big cockroach indeed I thought. And then I realised it was nothing of the sort. It was a rat.

For some reason there does not appear to be space for my views about rats

BOB MONKHOUSE

What's Funny About Animals?

o O o

I knew I'd met a rogue elephant when the ivory he sold me turned out to be bakelite.

I wrote that joke when I was eleven years old. My mother had just explained to me the pachydermatous allusion in the title of Geoffrey Household's novel *Rogue Male* and I was onto its comic potential like the joke-obsessed child I was. Bakelite was a pre-war kind of plastic.

In those days I thought all animals were very funny and most of my childhood jests and cartoons seemed to involve them. When a man on the wireless talked about 'milking a snake', another entry went into my exercise book:

Milking a snake can't be easy. How do you get the little bucket between its legs?

Throughout my adolescence I continued to add to my hand-written collection, making up simple jokes about tired kangaroos being out of bounds, swimming elephants never forgetting their trunks, newly wed rabbits going on a bunnymoon, ingrown hares, weeping hyenas, tarnished goldfish, teetotal newts, vertiginous lemmings, and, as sexual sophistication dawned, female deer passing the buck and randy squirrels putting it in a nutshell.

Today I turn the dog-eared pages of my notebooks, look back upon my youthful self and marvel that I was ever so naïve as to suppose that animals were something to laugh about. Life was soon to teach me otherwise.

The idea of owning an animal had always seemed quite barmy to me. Sam, the black family cat of my early youth, was the most independent creature I knew and, so far as I could tell, thought he owned us. As our proprietor he was very fair. As long as we provided him with food, drink and comfort, he allowed us complete freedom to the day he died chasing a fieldmouse across Bromley Road, Beckenham, under the wheels of a 227 bus to Penge. He was his own moggie to the end.

Notwithstanding my inability to grasp the concept of anyone actually possessing Sam or any other living creature, my parents bought me a tortoise and told me it was mine to keep. Of course it wasn't. It never gave the smallest acknowledgement of my existence, let alone recognition of my sovereignty.

Its raisin eyes showed no awareness as it snapped liplessly at lettuce, released gnarled droppings from its other end and staggered off pointlessly to anywhere and nowhere. You could paint the name 'Valerie' on its shell in ochre enamel – and I did – but it made not a ha'porth of difference to the thing's real identity which was about as interesting as that of a conker and not as much fun to play with.

Valerie was tucked up for the winter of 1938 in a shoebox full of straw and left to hibernate. We forgot all about her until the following June when my father and I were in the cupboard under the stairs looking for his tennis racquet. He found the shoebox, brought it out into the hall to look underneath the straw and shouted, 'Robert! You don't deserve to have nice things!'

I watched him toss Valerie's more-or-less vacant shell into the dustbin and felt sorry, not for Valerie but for myself. I had never asked to be a zookeeper. Thereafter no tortoise jokes appear in my schoolboy notebooks. There are no jokes about waxbills either.

The first I knew about them was the noise. I was just home

from school and taking off my overcoat and cap in our hall when I heard an unpleasant squeaking and clattering from behind the open door of the sitting room.

I peeked in and saw my mother beaming through her glasses and poking a finger between the bars of a large square birdcage on the sideboard. Within their prison bustled four small and nasty-looking birds with swollen red beaks and hard claws that rattled on the perches and swings. I watched them flutter and collide and splash water on the fruit bowl, their clowns' noses emitting horrid staccato beeps. 'Look, Robert,' she said. 'Here are your new pets. They're yours to keep.'

I knew what that meant: that I was saddled with the jobs of cleaning, watering and spending my weekly pocket money on millet and cuttlefish for these vile, hysterical intruders. Mine to keep? All the waxbills knew about me was my unwelcome proximity. I only had to enter the room for the little dunderheads to go into their regular frenzy routine, filling the cage with ear-splitting panic, feathers flying out everywhere and their high-pitched Morse Code signalling gormless alarm.

On 3 September 1939, Neville Chamberlain declared war and my father returned the rackety birds to the pet-shop preparatory to evacuating the family to West Worthing. I felt like writing Herr Hitler a fan letter.

In West Worthing I turned thirteen and my best friend at school presented me with three white mice in a wooden box with a glass front and a little wheel. I left its door open all night. The next morning two of the stupid things were still in there. I put them in a paper bag and surreptitiously released then at the back of a hardware and grain store in the high street. Mixed emotions: I felt like Lincoln freeing the slaves as an expression of selfish vandalism. Abandoning the white mice, however, had also been an act of self-definition. I knew now that I wanted nothing to do with captive creatures. I stuck firmly to this decision, politely refusing proffered gifts of puppies, budgerigars and hamsters. But years, as they pass, tend to weaken resolve and I was to fall victim twice more to the burden of responsibility that is Animal Magic. That is, if you can apply the word animal to Jackson's Tri-horns.

I was twenty-eight by now, leading a sportive company of entertainers in summer season at the Winter Gardens, Blackpool. My dresser was a dear old man called Harry who had a very special friend named Garth. One day Harry came to me in tears and told me that his special friend had gone off with another special friend who was apparently more special than Harry.

''E's scarpered with this lad half his age, just gone off just like that! Not a word, not a thank you, not a kiss-me'ow's-your-father. And what am I to do with 'is pets? I can't gie 'em an 'ome, Mr Munt'ouse, I've not got the faculties at my 'ouse. So I was wondering if you could see your way to – er – well, they're no trouble, I promise. Very quiet and quite valuable to them as likes 'em. A bit of food, a bit of warm, and they amuse theirselves really.'

Feebly resisting, I found myself giving a home to two of the ugliest reptiles I'd ever seen; triple-horned chameleons named Edward II and Gaveston. They were grisly lizards with swivelling eyes who moved hardly at all around an arrangement of leafless branches inside a huge glass cage which now rested on a low bench in my hired summer home. I was told that a constant temperature of eighty to ninety degrees was necessary. The mid-1957 weather was blustery and cool on the Fylde coast, so I bought a convection heater and left it permanently switched on in the spare room where the unnatural pair perched in implacable immobility.

Apart from the cost of maintaining this stifling heat in the room, there was a sickly smell, not from the scaly namesakes of the English king and his bit of rough but from their essential food.

I had to call in daily at a bait shop in Fleetwood for a tin of bluebottle maggots. Have you ever looked into a tin of bluebottle maggots? If you have you'd remember not to do it again and if you haven't, don't. It's Dante's flyblown inferno; a writhing pandemonium of three hundred off-white grubs with a single black dot at one end which may serve as maw or anus or both. Like simmering sour milk they squirm in unceasing agitation, horribly burrowing and surfacing under and over each other, vermiform souls in a frantic furnace, impelled by cruel nature to survive this crucible in order to achieve their eventual glory and become bluebottles. It doesn't half put you off all that reincarnation malarkey.

Gaveston was a natural marksman. Inside the glass case the bluebottles were born and began to buzz about. One would light within his range. His independently rotating eyes would fix upon it. His disgusting tongue would thicken his squamalose throat, then shoot out to its full nine inches, attaching a sticky globular tip to the insect, then reeling it in to be munched reflectively.

Edward II was a lousy shot and within three weeks he was lying in the bottom of the case having literally dropped off the twig. For the first time he changed colour. Still green but definitely pasty.

Gaveston stopped eating, a fatal loss of appetite which I at first attributed to grief but, as I later learned from the pet-shop proprietor who examined his corpse, was due to botweed. Good.

And so to my final, and I swear upon its finality, brush with the Wild and Wacky World of Wildlife. I adopted a chimpanzee.

Oh, I can sense your contempt. Here was I, aged thirty-three, a full-grown man with a history of pet death, reneging on all I had determined. I've no real defence either since my purpose was low, a cheap – well, cheapish – grab for publicity. I was in the twelfth month of a play at the Prince of Wales Theatre in London's West End and business was flagging. A publicist named Ben Lewis said, 'We need picture coverage. Picture editors like monkeys. For a few quid a week you can adopt a monkey at Regent's Park Zoo, pay for its keep. A Monkey for Monkhouse! Bob In the Monkey House! I don't know how I think 'em up.'

It turned out that all the primates at London Zoo were taken. 'Never fear, Chessington Zoo's got a pregnant chimp, going to drop it any day now. Bob's Bringing Up Baby Bonzo! I like it.'

I got to the zoo on the day the baby chimp was born. The two keepers responsible for the Chessington apes were both named Gus. They had removed the baby from its mother as a safety measure. The little creature was quite repulsive, lying unconscious in an oxygen tent as if drowned, its thin black hairs pasted to pinkish-grey skin.

'You can't pick him up yet, can he, Gus?' said Gus.

Pick him up? I felt ill just looking at him.

'But come back tomorrow and you can help to feed him, can't he, Gus?' said the other Gus.

The next day I posed for photographs holding the infant Kong, a name I'd offered in fun but which had been immediately adopted. I managed to manoeuvre a rubber teat into Kong's weak mouth and he ingested more milk and sugar water than he brought back up. I felt proud.

The next day I drove to the zoo again and waited till Kong wakened and I could feed him again. I though he looked a bit stronger. As I nursed him, I became aware of his mother looking at us from her cage about twelve feet away. She grinned at me and I felt encouraged.

Somehow I found myself at a loose end most days over the following weeks and made the daily trip to spend a few hours with Kong. He was still sickly but there was a new shine to his eyes and he could lift his head and grasp the feeding bottle with a promising energy. My depression over sagging receipts at our theatre box office had lifted also and my stage brother, young Michael Crawford, remarked on my restored involvement in my role. Business picked up too.

Just one month after Kong was born I drove to Chessington as usual. Caring for Kong was occupying most of my days and I was gratified that the little fellow was recognising me now and clinging to me while he slept after a feed. His mother's grins from her neighbouring cage had become wider than ever. Her unwanted offspring had mysteriously become my most absorbing concern and I arrived with a mixture of small fruits – grapes, cherries, currants – which I hoped might tempt him.

Both Guses – should that be Gusses, or for Latin scholars *GI* ? – met me at the gates with grim expressions. I got ready to summon up a joke to keep pain away. It wouldn't come and I was without defence.

My Kong was dead. On instructions from the zoo's director or some other, the little chap had been returned to his mother for nursing. She had killed him at once.

I thanked the keepers and drove away. I drove around all day and, for the first time in over a year, was late for my stage entrance that evening. To this day I can't remember where I went or what I did.

Since then I've composed thousands of jokes about various animals. It's unlikely that I'll ever learn to hate a rogue elephant or love one either. I'm never likely to have an emotional involvement with a giraffe or a polar bear or a golden eagle. Jokes about these clowns are still easy. I can do you a nice line in unicorn gags, for instance.

I just don't choose to joke about creatures mammalian, reptilian or avian with whom I have had personal contact but established no rapport whatsoever. They don't need me and I don't need them. The mere thought of their natural indifference robs me of the ability to laugh at them. You'll never hear me kidding about the total self-interest of tortoises, cage birds, tame mice or monochrome chameleons.

And I don't joke about chimpanzees either.

They can tear your heart out, these strange brutes. And if they teach you more about yourself than you ever knew, it's not intentional. They neither know nor care what you think of them. They're animals, that's all. Brutal, dreadful, irritating, selfish, silly, exposed, forsaken, hopeless nuisances . . .

Just like me.

PAUL HEINEY

A Pig Like Alice

○ ◯ ○

One of the wisest pieces of advice I was given when I first started to farm was that you should never keep animals of which you
are not fond. That is why, on my farm, you will find neither geese
nor goats. There are no geese because at the age of three I was
well and truly bitten by my great aunt Evelyn's gander, and given
time can still find the scar. I have loathed the hissing brutes ever
since. It is the arrogant way they attack without even pausing to
consider whether you be friend or foe; you need only appear
above their limited horizons for those forceful wings to start
beating and wispy pink tongues to waggle from within a wide-
open, sharpened and determined orange beak. I have no time for
geese.

I cannot stand goats either; or to be precise, cannot stand goat-
keepers. A macho acquaintance who dispensed wisdom freely
when perched on a bar-stool always warned me, tapping the side
of his nose as he did so, that if he ever saw a man order lager and
lime, he started to look for the handbag. Well, when I see goats I
look for sandals and a general air of mental instability. As for the

goats, they are wonderful scavengers when set to clearing a meadow of weeds, but desperately dangerous if ever allowed to go free. They destroy anything green that comes within range of those mean little eyes. Napalm on four legs. And they stink.

So why was it that the first farm animal I ever bought was a pig? Are they not equally odorous in their habits, noisy in their squealing and grunting, ruthless when deploying their powerful snouts? All these things are to a certain extent true; but I have to admit that in my case, love conquered all.

I fell for Alice the moment I saw her, although these days I prefer to admire her from afar, as I shall explain. She was plump, and although still girlish in many ways (her back view, with those high-heeled trotters, resembled nothing so much as a traditional barmaid in a short tight skirt), it was clear that she would mature into a fine figure of a sow. She was gloriously rounded, with ears so finely textured that to make a silk purse out of them would have been an insult; her nose twitched in a coy way and her tightly curled tail spoke volumes for the gallons of sheer health that she carried around in her ever-expanding frame. And she was black; as dark as a newly dug lump of coal and agile as a polished cannon-ball. She was a distinguished member of a rare breed of pig called, appropriately, the Large Black.

Like many old breeds of farm animal that we have consigned to history in the search for more profit, the Large Black pig has been left behind in small numbers, to be savoured only by connoisseurs who know what real pigs should be like and, it must be admitted, what real pig-meat should taste like. I doubt we could ever marry our dear Alice to applied sauce and slice her for dinner, but we have tasted pork from black pigs and I apologise if the juices dribble down your chin when I describe the sweetness of the meat, the moistness of it and the crackling that splinters into a thousand taste-loaded missiles as you bite into it. Do not believe for one minute that farming these days produces better food than fifty years ago. It is merely more plentiful. The price of the plenty has been the flavour.

But none of these burning issues occupies many of Alice's thoughts. She spends her winter days in a sty and dozes quietly from one meal to the next like an old lady passing away her days in a hotel in Bognor. But in the summer she goes out to grass and her first task is to destroy it all. She gets her head so far down to the ground that her long floppy ears cover her eyes completely to shut out the world, and then with her muscular snout she digs and digs. I am not certain she ever finds what she is looking for, which may only have been a worm in the first place, for she soon tires and ambles into the shade to dream of the next meal. If it is very hot, she digs herself a hole to lie in and if we are feeling kind we will fill it with water and then she wallows in her own little mud-bath, refining her blood, as happy as any beauty could wish to be. It is heart-breaking to think of the way pigs are often kept, indoors, in intensive conditions, when it is clear even to the untutored eye that they adore their freedom.

But Alice is not without her faults. She is prolific, and on occasions has given birth to litters of thirteen piglets. This poses something of a problem for she has only eleven teats, having lost one in some accident in her youth. But having two more mouths to feed than there are places at the table is no problem for her; she organises a rota and makes sure the piglets stick to it; and if one gets left out it may be seen going round the teats after the others have finished, mopping up the leftovers like a drunk trying to squeeze a drop of ale from a beermat. But when Alice tires of her litter, she does not disguise the fact. She has learnt to sit, like a dog, in such a position that all her teats are flat against the ground and no hungry little piglet can get anywhere near them. Oh yes, she is a cunning old girl.

And somewhat forward on occasions. When it is her time to come on heat, or 'on song' as the old boys round here call it, it is no time to linger and listen to her aria. She will get alarmingly playful, take a lump of trouser in her mouth and rub her head against your shin, hardly disguising the fact that should you be looking for a good time, Alice is your girl. The first time this happened, I found it rather disturbing to have a quarter-ton of black pig running at me with lips pursed and, had I hung around long enough to find out, I dare say a dab or two of perfume behind the ears. I was over the fence as if fired from a rocket. But I still love you Alice, and hope you understand why I sometimes prefer to gaze upon you from afar.

LIBBY PURVES

Ram Raid

o O o

I am standing out here in this blackberry bush, holding onto this
rope. Not, you understand, as I write: the rope is jerking too
much to write, even had I had time to bring a notebook. The jerking is to do with the ram, which is on the other end of the rope
on a slip-knot. It has had me over twice, the fleecy hooligan.
Each time it was only the tightening of the noose around its horrible neck which quietened it for a moment so I could struggle
back to my feet.

No, all I am doing at the moment is hanging on grimly, and
tugging, and falling over occasionally, and thinking. Thinking
that one day I am going to write this all down, whatever he says.
OK, OK, I am not the farming writer of the family. This is his
farm, not mine [see page 51]. He invented it, he works it, he
knows the right things to shout at sheepdogs. But I live here too,
I am an appendage, I am the Farmer's Wife. So sometimes I end
up spending forty-five minutes of valuable creative literary time
standing in a bush with a rope and a ram, while distant curses and
hysterical bleating echo around his forty acres.

It is always the sheep that start something. In our early days of sheepkeeping, they got out so frequently that on one occasion Paul tried to ring some friends one evening, then came into the sitting room saying conversationally, 'They're out.' Half-asleep in front of the television, I leapt to my feet, groping for a stick and shouting 'Where? Where are the woolly bastards this time?'

This morning, what happened was that a mob of giggling ewe-lambs broke out of their enclosure like St Trinian's girls on the rampage, and inadvertently trespassed in the field where three elderly rams were chewing thoughtfully and remembering past glories, in the Garrick-club way which rams affect outside the breeding season. Well, we all know what trouble women can cause in a chaps' club. Inflamed by the arrival of these appalling Lolitas – most of them their own daughters and granddaughters – the rams began a campaign of serious sexual harassment, spotted by my horrified farmer spouse from the other side of the land. Bellowing to me to leave my carefully crafted 800 words for the book pages, he galloped up to the scene of debauchery with his faithful sheepdog, rounded up the marauding girls, and kicked two of the rams into a handy pen.

Not, however, the biggest ram. Throwing the rope around its neck ('Never underestimate the usefulness of asphyxia in animal management,' he gasped) and handing me the other end, he departed in pursuit of the dog and the ewes, by now streaming away across some sprouting corn. He could not shut the field-gate behind him in the rush; I cannot get to the gate without the ram escaping and starting out in lustful pursuit.

All I can do is – well, be. In the bramble bush, clutching my rope, and aiming the occasional kick at the woolly chest when it stops pulling and tries pushing. Until he gets back from wherever he is trying to incarcerate the lambs, I dare not let go. 'Stay put,' were his last words to me. Well, not quite the last. 'Thank God,' he added chivalrously as he panted away, 'you've got a bit of weight to hold him if he gets stroppy.' It is nice to be appreciated. We farmers' wives do like these little compliments. We glow.

So the mind wanders, and wonders, as the distant cries and bleats echo across the farm. I know what he is doing, because I have seen it before. He is playing a highly complicated form of woolly snooker. This is what you have to do, with sheep. They exist in a state of permanent, mild, probably not unpleasant panic. They are not genuinely frightened of the dog – when they have new lambs, they round on him and chase him half a mile, tail between his legs – but, like schoolgirls shrieking at a cheeky biker, they rather enjoy pretending to be in a dithering panic over this mild, unassuming, rather nervous sheepdog: veering and skittering away from the course of his run.

The shepherd, of course, is meant to be controlling that run, with deafening cries of COOM BYE! and HOWAAY! But the matter is not straightforward: if there is an open gate and you drive sheep towards it, they will scatter in panic and fall into the ditches and hedges on either side, too stupid to get the point. So you aim them at some solid obstruction, calculating that they will then ricochet off it and stream through the gate before it dawns on them that this is what you wanted all the time.

By the sound of it, there have been a good few ricochets and rebounds on the way back to their proper field. When it goes quiet, I will know that he is on his way back to rescue me from ram duty. Perhaps.

Of course, something else could have happened to distract his attention. Glancing through the hedge at the other sheep, he might notice that one of them has its legs pointing skywards. This indicates stranding. The woollier they get in the early summer, the more likely they are to roll onto their backs like beetles and get stuck. Twelve hours of this, and they die. The caring shepherd's task is to give them a shove with his boot, so that they get up and trot sheepishly away. If they have been down too long, you have to pour a pint of cooking oil down their throat, which causes a massive eructation of wind from both ends, and an instant cure. Once, sent running in panic to such a scene, I grabbed the classy olive oil, the stuff with the clove of garlic steeping in it. The sheep's vast belch, to anyone who happened to be holding it in an intimate armlock at the time, was reminiscent of many a Mediterranean holiday: even to the disturbing undertones of Feta cheese beyond the oil and garlic. It was a complete kebab of a belch, which returns to me sometimes in

Greek restaurants, resulting in a remarkable loss of appetite.

Rambo the ram has given up now, and is lying down, sadly forgetting the erotic ambitions of half an hour ago. A ewe is only a ewe, he mutters to himself; but a mouthful of grass is solid comfort. Soon the ordeal will be over, and I can get back to the word processor and tap out some polished phrases of my book review.

Here comes Farmer Heiney, shutting the gate, releasing us from our bondage. But why is he not beaming in relief? Why is he still waving that stick and shouting 'Hurry up!'? What is going on? What does he mean, 'The sheep shorted the electric fence and let the pigs out'?

RICHARD GORDON

The Incredible Talking Dog

o ◯ o

The literary man and his dog went to mow many a lush meadow. What four-legged friends were the prototypes of Bill Sykes's Bull's-eye, of Nana, of Rab, of Toby, of the Hound of the Baskervilles and the dog who did nothing in the night-time? Byron patted his faithful Boatswain, Pope his Bounce, Charles Lamb his Dash, Beverley Nichols licensed Mr Sponge and P G Wodehouse kennelled a pedigreed pack. Schopenhauer philosopically took his dog walkies for two hours every afternoon at four, however awful the weather in Frankfurt.

A dog is literally vital for a literary man. The *métier* is antagonistic to healthy living. The literary man can stay watching TV in bed until the morning chat shows are over. He need not shave, nor even wash. He can get as pissed as he likes at lunchtime. And he need never leave home at all if it looks like rain.

A dog is an incitement to exercise more powerful than a newly bought static bike. A wife's imploring look of 'please take me out' can pass cruelly unnoticed to a man in unsociable mood. A dog's, never.

For forty years I have lived in bosky, doggy Bromley, a London suburb between the nationally famous names of Crystal Palace and Biggin Hill. Every afternoon I walk in the 300 acres of Petts Wood. This is a leafy memorial to Bromley's son William Willett (1856–1915), who unbeseechedly lightened our darkness. It displays his memorial sundial, a granite plinth with a massive gnomon set to summer time (if ten minutes slow) and chiselled *Horas non numero nisi aestivi*, the classics still being alive in Bromley.

Petts Wood supports profuse wildlife – squirrels, rabbits, foxes, flashers. Its birds, as evidenced by walkers with binoculars, are worth watching. It is pierced by Botany Bay Lane, suggesting an old connection of the locals with Australia. There is a Lovers' Lane, its mossy banks strewn, in warmer weather, with delicate emblems of satisfied passion. Petts Wood was viewed from 1871 to 1873 by Napoleon III, who lived there with the Empress Eugénie in the local golf club (they did not play). Over these forty years of wandering in Petts Wood, with a tape-recorder snug in my pocket to preserve literary thought, I have written forty books and worn beyond repair countless pairs of shoes, six Lock's caps and twelve dogs.

As each day's walk for me and my dog is six and a half miles, this makes $2,374\frac{1}{2}$ miles a year, which, the circumference of the earth being 24,901 miles, means that I have now circled the globe thrice and I am passing the Taj Mahal on my way home for the fourth time. In the springtime when I was last between Salt Lake City and San Francisco, I acquired Yorick; Brutus and Cleopatra having ascended to the Elysian kennels.

Yorick was a scion of the Battersea dynasty. He was short haired, black and white, stubby-tailed, a foot and a half long, shaped like an antique brandy cask on short legs, with pointed ears, a long muzzle and a tight mouth. He had comfortably settled into our suburban home when we discovered that he could understand every work that we uttered.

In the evening, Yorick would sit between master and mistress before the smokeless fire, his head turning to register such items of domestic conversation as: 'Why the hell don't we change channels?' with brisk repeated nods. Outbursts of opinion common in literary households, like: 'This Booker Prize novel is pretentious codswallop,' or 'Gold knows what we're going to do for money,' had Yorick to his paws, barking and jumping several inches off the kelim hearthrug in enthusiastic agreement.

I shortly suspected that my dumb friend passionately wished to join the chat. His lips would twitch, his teeth snap, a thin whine quivered from his throat, his body shook in articulatory frustration. Then, one morning in the Charing Cross Road, I wandered as literary men do, into a secondhand bookshop. I found my hand on *Ye Mistick Dogges*, by Benedict Cullpepper, who was a contemporary of Nostradamus (1503–66). On the thick yellowed pages I read:

It is given to divers small plump dogges the power of human speech, for a nonce at ye chime of midnight on Midsummer's Eve, if mayhap the dogge prowls amid the faerie spirits and such as flit that night within the woods.

I paid whatever the bookseller asked, hurried to Charing Cross Station and rattled excitedly to Bromley. It was 19 June. A day to go.

On Midsummer's Eve, when we had cleared away our suburban tea, I paced impatiently between our privet hedges awaiting 9.21 pm, when Whitaker's Almanack told me that darkness would fall. To calm myself, I had some long, summer-iced Scotch-and-sodas, and thoughtfully filled and refilled Yorick's drinking-bowl. At sunset, I went indoors and played the disc of *Midsommarvaka*. At eleven, I restlessly took the lead, and we left along the sedate lamplit streets for Petts Wood.

If any dog looked charged with the power of speech, to be detonated by a mystical time-switch, it was Yorick. But what *would* he say? 'Four-Feet trotting behind' must have some intriguing, enlightening, philosophical opinion to pass about the elevated beings whose heels scrape before his wet nose. Or might he give some startling insight into the dog's universe of subtle smells? Or perhaps a snatch of doggerel?

We were deep in the wood. The moon shone vividly. There was a Titania up every tree. An owl in the distance took its cue. Further off, rang the chimes of Bromley parish church . . .

He spoke!

60

He said: 'I don't know about you, mate, but I don't half want to lift my leg.'

Alas, poor Yorick! In the excitement, I had forgotten the bloody tape-recorder.

TIM RICE

How Now!
A Singing Beast?

o ◯ o

The animal kingdom has been the inspiration for many popular songs over the years. Rare indeed is the year-end Top Forty without some reference to fauna. Few species have escaped the grasp of composers; from the early days of the British charts (first published in November 1952) a lyric about our furry, feathered or even scaly friends has often kept its writer in cat litter for decades. What follows is merely a quick look at the biggest livestock sellers of all.

Barely had the UK charts got going when Guy Mitchell took an animal, or at least parts of an animal, to Number One via his immortal rendering of 'She Wears Red Feathers'. Guy reigned supreme for four weeks in March and April 1953 before being sensationally replaced by another pinion-inspired masterpiece, 'Broken Wings' by the Stargazers. It seemed as if nothing could break the animal stranglehold on the best-sellers when the Stargazers were in turn knocked off their perch by Lita Roza's unforgettable 'How Much Is That Doggie In The Window?' By this time 37.5% of the Number Ones of all time had featured animals. Inevitably there was a backlash and unless you assume Eddie Fisher was portraying a devoted mutt when he emoted 'I'm Walking Behind You' later in Coronation Year, there was no non-human mega-smash until Andy Williams and 'Butterfly' in May 1957.

Williams's triumph was the first half of an insect double that year as Buddy Holly's group, the Crickets, scored their first hit (and only number one) in November – 'That'll Be The Day'. Nothing in the six-legged or even four-legged stakes made it so big for the best part of another two years, when Russ Conway had a chart-topper with equine connotations (at least we must hope it only related to horses): the celebrated 'Side Saddle'. 1960 saw the first wild animal Number One via Johnny Preston and 'Running Bear' which grizzly platter remained the only bestial head of the sixties hit parade until insects came back with a buzz via 1962's 'Nut Rocker' courtesy of B Bumble and the Stingers. 1962 was also the year that saw the greatest insect group of them all make its chart debut: the Beatles, a name inspired by the Crickets, although it was not until the following year that John, Paul, George and Ringo notched the first of their seventeen Number Ones between 1963 and 1970. None of the seventeen titles had obvious animal links, but while they were the kings of pop, many other acts and big hits did.

In July 1964 a band whose name paid tribute to more things non-human than any other, the Animals, made it all the way with 'The House of the Rising Sun', The Honeycombs built on B Bumble's apiarist legacy with 'Have I the Right'. A great year for dumb creatures wound up with the Beatles' closest rivals, the Rolling Stones, striking a blow for poultry with 'Little Red Rooster'. A new bird age, reminiscent of Guy Mitchell and the Stargazers, but this time incorporating the entire beast, was upon us. 1965 saw the Byrds take flight with 'Mr Tambourine Man'. The American quintet's success was a major factor in encouraging the British quintet Manfred Mann to release their triumphant 'Pretty Flamingo' the following summer.

It took a brave hand to break away from the feathered trend, but that is just what the Monkees did in early 1967 via a string of hit singles, notably 'I'm a Believer', and a TV series. But when their popularity finally began to wane, the birds came back bigger than ever thanks to Fleetwood Mac's 'Albatross' at the beginning of 1969. The next animal Number One, in 1971, was yet another strictly for the birds, 'Chirpy Chirpy Cheep Cheep' by Middle of the Road, but despairing dog-lovers finally came in from the cold after 19 years when teen idol Donny Osmond took man's best fried back to the summit of popular taste when he scored with 'Puppy Love'. Better yet, David Cassidy did the same a year later with 'The Puppy Song', with only Lieutenant Pigeon's 'Mouldy Old Dough' briefly threatening a return of bird supremacy between the two canine biggies.

1974 saw Mud's 'Tiger Feet' bring an endangered species to the top for the first time which was what animal hits then became. Over four years passed before the Boomtown Rats and 'Rat Trap' became the first case of an act with an animal name reaching the top with an animal song. In 1979 Art Garfunkel's 'Bright Eyes', from the movie *Watership Down* was about rabbits, though not obviously so. Things improved as the new decade got under way. Continuing the record world's profitable infatuation with insect names, Adam and the Ants were the biggest pop act of the early eighties. Tight Fit paid tribute to the king of the beasts with 'The Lion Sleeps Tonight' in March 1982, and in September Survivor made it two in eight years for that particular cat with 'Eye of the Tiger'. 1983 had Boy George and Culture Club outshining all others for six weeks with 'Karma Chameleon'. Then followed three bleak years until the farmyard ruled the roost for three weeks in 1986 with Spitting Image's 'The Chicken Song'.

Recent years have been unexciting for animal-lovers although the Pet Shop Boys enjoyed no less than four number ones from 1985-8. Jive Bunny had three, all within five months in 1989, Turtles were at the top via 'Turtle Power' and Partners in Kryme (1990) and insects yet again courtesy of U2 and 'The Fly' (1991). Nothing major since, which indicates that a 1953 or 1964 type explosion of bestiality may well be in the wings, so to speak.

The above survey has, to coin a phrase, barely scratched the surface of wildlife in the charts. For every Number One hit there have been a dozen lesser successes, not to mention ventures such as the Singing Dogs and the Tweets. Birds and dogs have clearly been the best bet for zoological chart-topping although the ultimate combination of these two subjects, 'Bird Dog' by the Everly Brothers, stalled at number two in 1958. Perhaps today's songwriters should stick to human passion after all.

BARRY NORMAN

I Know Two Things About the Horse

o O o

They came home, wife and two daughters, late in the afternoon, flushed with the triumph of a successful mission. 'We've got a horse,' they chorused, like a bunch of superannuated racing tipsters.

This was the first I had heard of horses and I failed to share their enthusiasm. 'We do not need a horse,' I said. 'We have no room for a horse. Look around you. The two dogs and the two cats won't let it in the house and the guinea pigs have occupied the garden.'

Wives, however, are rarely deterred by such trivial objections for they always have a trump card up their sleeves. 'Ah, yes,' said mine, playing what she clearly perceived to be her ace, 'but think of the manure.'

'I am thinking of the manure,' I said. 'I can think of little else. Piles of it. All over our minuscule back lawn.'

'No, no,' she said, 'don't think lawn, think rose bushes. Manure on the rose bushes. We'll have a wonderful display.'

I directed her attention towards the flower bed. 'Out there,' I said, 'we have two rose bushes. Count them. Two. This is suffi-cient reason to buy a horse?'

'We'll get more. We'll get lots and our roses will be the envy of the whole village. Right. What do you want for tea?'

The horse turned up a few days later, a palomino with an atti-tude, the result very possibly of the fact that it was distinctly on the short side and only just scraped in as a horse rather than a pony.

It was, inevitably, female. In our house all animals are female or, if they don't start out that way, they are rendered the next best thing by being immediately neutered in the interests of creating a testosterone-free zone. There are times, I may tell you, when I wonder how I myself have managed to escape this process and there are other times when I wonder whether *I have* managed to escape this process.

'Dad,' said our elder daughter, for whom the animal had been acquired, 'this is Loner. Give her a pat.' Loner and I regarded each other warily. I stretched out a hand; she bared her teeth and that was about as far, and as affectionate, as the introduction got.

The good news was that Loner was not to lodge with us but with some friends down the road who had a stable and a pad-dock. She was duly installed there; essential items such as jodh-purs, boots, saddle, bridle and hard hat, to say nothing of some-thing called an egg-butt snaffle (which, in my innocence, I ini-tially took to be the name of her riding instructor. Egbert Snaffle? Well, it's possible. Unlikely, yes, but possible) were acquired for our daughter; and I settled back to await the first promised load of manure, this being, as far as I could see, the only benefit like-ly to accrue to me from the entire transaction.

The Americans, as you may know, have a crude but graphic phrase: 'Shit happens.' Loner, unfortunately, appears never to have heard of it because in her case it didn't happen – ever.

We have, between us, supported this animal for twenty years, in comfort if not indeed in luxury, and in all that time our rose bush-es, increased in number now to at least six, have never benefited by so much as an ounce of manure. Deprived of this essential nutrition they loll, as they have always done, wimpishly about the garden, jeered at even by strangers as nerds among rose bushes.

After the first few weeks as I studied the horse's financial balance sheet – expenditure: plenty; income, in the form of manure: nil – I called a family conference to discuss the situation.

'Is it possible,' I asked, 'that she's selling the stuff privately to someone else? Or could it be that a gang of international horse-manure thieves is going around?'

They glanced about them nervously. We were in a field near our house and Loner, saddled and otherwise accoutred for action, was lurking nearby. 'Let's not talk about it in her presence,' they said. 'Tell you what, why don't you ride her, get to know her?'

It was many years since I had ridden, but if my climbing on Loner's back would help release her bowels, I was game. Wife and daughters clustered round to give me a hand, several hands. 'One, two, three,' they said and heaved. Slowly, as in a dream, I sailed over the saddle and landed in a heap on the other side. My friend Julian, who was also present, walked away, shaking, with his handkerchief in his mouth.

The second time was better. I got on, the horse started walking, the family cheered. Confident now, I dug my heels in, Loner broke into a trot, I looked back and waved – and at this point the bloody animal came to an emergency stop. A moment later I was in a heap again on one side of a wire fence while Loner studied me thoughtfully from the other side. Julian was in a heap as well, rolling about and drumming his heels on the turf, while the family, apparently smitten with some kind of collective ague, had turned their backs on me and were clutching each other.

Since the fence was unclimbable and the nearest gate was about half a mile away I did what any self-respecting man would have done – I turned on my heel and walked home with a dignified limp.

That was the end of it, really. Oh, Loner is still about but we don't attempt to fraternise any more.

Occasionally, when my daughter rides her past our house, I enquire after the current state of her digestive system but the answer is always the same – 'Sorry, dad, no news.'

I've pretty well stopped worrying about it now for, as I see it, there are only two possible solutions to this puzzle. Either there is, somewhere in our country, a concealed manure mountain of incalculable value. Or, and this is the thought that gives me the greater pleasure, Loner is the only horse in equine history to have suffered from chronic, unrelieved, lifelong constipation. After the expense and discomfiture she had caused me, it's the least she deserves.

KEITH WATERHOUSE

All Their Yesterday

o O o

Two elderly mayflies are hovering on a rain-puddle. They were born around seven yesterday morning. It is now getting on for two am. In a few hours they will pass away. It has been a long life.

'It is not what it was like when we were lads,' grumbles the first mayfly. 'There was none of this total darkness same as what you get now.'

'It was all light and sunny,' the second mayfly agrees. 'I can remember when you could see to the end of the road.'

'You're going back a bit there, Cyril,' says the first mayfly.

'I blame the Russians, Walter. You cannot tell me all them nuclear tests up Siberia do not have an effect on the daylight.'

'Artificial lighting they have, these days.'

'Street lamps,' says the second mayfly with scorn. 'Cheap Japanese technology.'

'You never saw artificial lighting when we were young,' says the first mayfly. 'We didn't need it. You got your light from the sun, and if the sun went behind a cloud, you did without.'

The second mayfly says: 'Street lamps! These youngsters today don't know they're born.'

'No, there was nothing like that in them days. And there was no glowworms to gawp at for minutes on end, neither. Isn't that right, Cyril?'

'Too true, Walter,' says the second mayfly. 'We had to make our own amusements.'

The first mayfly cackles reminiscently: 'Do you remember the time we flew into that cow-swamp?'

The second mayfly scratches its head. 'By bloody hell, Walter, you aren't half trotting down Memory Lane with that one! You're going back to ten past three, aren't you?'

'Either ten past three else a quarter to four – I forget. But one thing I'll never forget is chasing that blonde mayfly with the big thrusting wings through them bullrushes. A right little cracker she was. I wonder where she is now.'

'In the Old Mayflies' Home, most likely,' says the second mayfly unkindly. 'She was a bit long in the tooth, you know, Walter. She was twelve hours old if she were a minute.'

'I like them mature,' says the first mayfly wistfully.

There is a tranquil silence. The time clock in the street lamp overhead clicks, and then the lamp switches itself off.

'Do you know what? Cyril,' says the first mayfly. 'I can't see my flaming antennae in front of my face. I reckon I need glasses.'

'You've got to expect it at our age,' says the second mayfly. 'We're not getting any younger.'

'Still,' the first mayfly ruminates, 'we've had a good run for our money, Cyril. I reckon it was a golden age, what we lived through.'

'It's them what's just starting out that I feel sorry for,' says the second mayfly. 'I mean to say, look at the uncertain times they're living in. Fancy growing up in the pitch darkness with the constant threat of the owl hanging over you. No wonder we get juvenile delinquency.'

'And the frog menace, Cyril,' says the first mayfly. 'Don't under estimate the frog menace.'

'I wasn't including conventional weapons, Walter. There's

been a frog menace for as long as there's been mayflies.'

'Maybe so,' says the first mayfly. 'Maybe so. But at least we could see the buggers.'

The second mayfly says: 'I've heard tell that in hundreds and hundreds of minutes from now, it should get light again. Something to do with the ice-cap shifting, I believe.'

'We won't live to see it lad. We'll be dead and buried by then.'

'Any road,' says the second mayfly, 'I've seen all I want to see. We've had some smashing times when you think about it, Walter.'

'Messing about on the council reservoir, eh?' remembers the first mayfly with a faraway look in its eyes. 'Mile after mile of shimmering water. I wonder if it's still there.'

'They'll have filled it in for development by now,' says the second mayfly.

'It seems like only yesterday, Walter.'

'It WAS only yesterday, you silly old fool,' the second mayfly says, but fondly.

DANNIE ABSE

Florida

o O o

Not one poem about an animal, she said,
in five, six volumes of poetry,
not one about The Peaceable Kingdom.
An accusation. Was she from the RSPCA?
Your contemporaries have all composed
inspired elegies for expired beasts;
told of salmon flinging themselves up
the sheer waterfall; cold crows,
in black rags, loitering near motorways;
parables of foxes and pheasants,
owls and voles, mice and moles,
cats, bats, pigs, pugs, snails, quails;
so why can't you write one, just one *haiku*?
Oh, I said, Oh! – then wondered if she knew
the story of the starving dowager.

The lady looked solemn as No.
Well, during the French Revolution,

the dowager, becoming thinner and thinner,
invited other lean aristocrats to dinner.
That night the guests saw (I continued)
slowly roasting on a rotating spit
the dowager's own poodle, Fido,
who proved to be most succulent.
So they made a feast of it.
Afterwards, the dowager sighed,
fingering the pearls about her neck,
sighed and said in noble French,
(I translate) What a damn shame Fido
isn't alive to eat up all those nice
crunchy bones left upon the plate.

My story over, I waited for applause. We'd
never cease from crying, she said,
if *one* insect could relate its misery.
Quite, I said, looking at my paws.
In Florida I saw a floating log
change and chase and swallow up
a barking dog. Hell, I said, an alligator?
A museum snake, too, in Gainesville,
Murder City, I can't forget,
poor black priapus in an empty case
lifting up its head for food not there.
With your gift I'd make a poem out of that.
So try, she said, do try and write
a creature poem and call it *Florida*.
I closed my eyes and she receded.

I thought of tigers and of Blake,
I thought of Fido and his bones.
No, no, she cried, think of Florida.
I saw the hotels of Miami Beach,
I heard waves collapsing ceaselessly.
No, no, she said, think again, think
of Florida, its creature Kingdom.
Like a TV screen my imagination
lit up to startle the ghost of Blake

with my own eidetic ads for Florida:
first, that black frustrated snake erect,
then two grapefruit inside a brassiere.
Open your eyes, the lady screamed, *wake up*.
I'm a poor bifurcated animal, I apologised.
Eagle beagle, bug grub, boar bear.

DONALD TRELFORD

Bushwhackers

o ○ o

The tsetse fly and the kudu bull are doubtless well acquainted
with each other, in ways one need not go into here. But why
should either be acquainted with me? I'll tell you. And while I'm
on about it, I might as well tell you about the snakes, and the lion
too.

All this happened thirty years ago on my real-life African
safari. I was out there editing a newspaper for Roy (later Lord)
Thomson in a country then called Nyasaland and about to
become Malawi. Before I left London on my exotic assignment
(I was only twenty-five), the Canadian press magnate summoned
me to his office to say farewell. Shaking my hand and pulling me
close to his thick pebble glasses, he drawled: 'You make a dollar
for me, boy, and I'll make a dollar for you.'

After a year of narrow scrapes and adventures, including finding a new-born black baby wrapped in a bundle of old newsprint
on the doorstep of my editorial office and racing British corre-
spondents down Zomba mountain by car in pitch darkness while
moderately drunk (the two incidents were not connected) – not

to mention the time the president, Dr Hastings Kamuzu Banda, pointed a finger at me and yelled, 'Keep out of my politics, white man!' – my wife and I decided to take the visiting parents-in-law on a trip to Zimbabwe, then still Southern Rhodesia.

The women went by plane to Harare, then called Salisbury, a neat colonial town with jacaranda trees, bougainvillaea and frangipani. The old man and I drove the car south through Mozambique, a journey of over 400 miles on dirt roads through bush country which, we had been warned, was filled with Frelimo guerrilla fighters.

When we came to the Zambezi river at Tete, we persuaded villagers to lift the car bodily onto a precarious raft and row it across. It was a hazardous trip, with the raft lurching dangerously over fast-flowing waters swollen by the rains. Apart from that and a puncture, which eager Africans helped us to mend, we seemed to have avoided the dangers we had been warned about.

Then, in the middle of nowhere, we came to a roadblock manned by four ragged men holding rifles and machine guns. We were directed down a track towards a big wooden barn. When I tried to protest, they waved their weapons in what I took to be a threatening gesture, so I shut up.

Armed guards unlocked the barn and beckoned the vehicle inside. We were ordered out, told to close our eyes, put our hands on our heads and turn round to face the wall. This is it, I thought. My father-in-law, who had served in the Flanders trenches and seen most of his friends killed at Passchendaele, told me afterwards that he had never felt so scared in his life.

What happened next was quite surreal. We and the car were all sprayed – not with the Valentine's Day massacre bullets we were expecting, but with what turned out to be tsetse fly repellent. It was an official tsetse control post. They waved us on our way with a smile. We didn't smile back.

In Salisbury we joined the ladies and drove on next day to Bulawayo, this time on a first-class road all the way. Nevertheless, I was tired after the Mozambique experience and agreed to let my wife have a spell at the wheel while I dozed over a book. We were close to our first stop, Wankie game reserve.

Suddenly there was a scream, both of voices and brakes, and the car lurched across the road, almost out of control. I woke up to see the most terrifying sight – a huge animal racing across the front of the car, on a seemingly unavoidable collision course. At 85 mph, there was only one possible outcome from that scenario.

Then, as if on wings, the animal took off like a Christmas reindeer, sailing over the car just as we were about to hit it. In fact, it hit the top of the car a sickening crack with its hoof and disappeared into the trees on the other side of the road. We staggered to a halt and sat for several minutes in silent meditation.

Eventually I got out to inspect the damage. The hoof had made an indentation about six inches above the windscreen. In other words, had the animal waited another second before launching itself on that death-defying leap, it would have crashed through the glass, blinding the driver, and we would surely have been written off against one of the trees at the side of the road.

We worked out later from pictures that it must have been a kudu bull. There were other recorded instances of them leaping over cars. The damage to the car cost £25 to repair. I'll never know what price the animal paid for saving our lives.

Ah yes, the snakes. As if he hadn't had enough of an adventure holiday already, my father-in-law suddenly found that he attracted them wherever he went.

He took a walk in the grounds of our house and a snake appeared through the stones at his feet and, mercifully, sped away. He went to the *chimbuzi*, the local word for the primitive loo, and a snake escaped when he lifted the lid. He threw some paper into a wastepaper basket and a snake crawled out and slid under the door. When we went for the weekend to Lake Nyasa to stay in a thatched hut on the beach, one fell out of a tree as he was walking under it.

My only direct contact with a snake came on a squash court we had in the garden. While I was playing the Reuters correspondent, a mamba fell from the thatched roof onto the court between us. Without even thinking, I bashed it in half with the side of my racket, hurled the remains through the door and turned back to continue the game.

The Reuters man, who had witnessed countless dangers in the field, had spread himself against the wall, white as a sheet. He could hardly speak, but finally muttered: 'You could do that to *people*.'

None of us was hurt in these incidents, but more than once the dog had venom spat in its eye, which my wife washed out with cold tea.

The dog had a rough time all round, especially at the lake. At night we could hear dog-eating hyenas crying in the hills behind, and doubtless so could he. The biggest night noise of all came from a lion, whose roar echoed round the bay. One night there was no roar, but in the ominous silence of the night we heard footsteps padding round the hut.

The dog whimpered in terror. I looked nervously at the 18-inch gap at the top of the door and wondered if a lion could slither through it. The lion, or whatever it was, started scratching at the door, then finally moved on. We heard next day that it had dragged off an African from the neighbouring village.

Maureen Lipman

It Shouldn't Happen to a Pet

o O o

I've never had a dog. As such. We didn't have any as children because they were not Dralon-friendly. One Saturday night my dad brought home a pup that someone had brought into the shop, probably in lieu of payment for a hacking jacket or a bale of Terylene mix. The pup was black and white and had already shown its aversion to Morris Oxfords by sprinkling the passenger seat halfway down Anlaby Road.

My mother took one look at him and did the only thing a woman of mature sensibilities could do under such circumstances: she had hysterics. Furnishing fabrics – the life expectancy and spiralling costs thereof – were brought into play. Axminster carpets were invoked, mounds of shedding hair touched upon. Mention was made more than once of, 'Who'd end up feeding it? Who'd have to schlep it for walks?' and, most pertinent of all, 'Who'd be cleaning up its never-ending lorryloads of "you known what"?' This led to finger-pointing at certain inhabitants of the house who never lifted them (fingers, that is) or cleaned out jet-black rings from baths, or even whitened their own plimsolls!

The innocent victims of these slanderous accusations began to bleat their protests. Their protests turned into full-scale demos. Satchels were flung. Doors slammed. Minor bashings ensued. 'S'not fair,' they wailed. 'S'like everything else in this house!' Everybody in their entire class, their entire school, the whole world and Hessle Foreshore had a dog. Some had five! And terrapins! How could the accused possibly learn a sense of responsibility if they had nothing to be responsible for? Of course they'd clean up after it . . . or . . . they'd train it to do it in the garden. O-oh, bad move . . . hadn't the garden just been nicely asphalted over to prevent other dogs from popping in, uninvited, to drop off their calling cards? *Cack On My Asphalt,* a slim volume by a women never parted from her Domestos bottle, sprang to mind.

It was over – bar the cowering. The puppy cowered, Dad cowered, we cowered. A coward would have cowered against such determined opposition. The dog dematerialised. Dad sulked for a few days, his tail between his legs. Mother told the same story with magnificent additions over the phone for twenty-four hours. My brother was eventually lured back with egg and chips and red jelly. I stayed in my bedroom, sucking the place where they'd nearly hit me until it turned into a hideous blood blister which took weeks to heal. That'd show 'em.

Of course, I may not have been good dog material. I may never know. I was always scared stiff of Alsatians. There was a short cut through to the back of the houses that entailed passing a fence, behind which prowled next-door-but-two's Alsatian. He had one job in life. To bark, and he was bloody good at it. I can still feel my heart exploding as I tiptoed the first few feet, then at the first sounds of his jaw opening, ran like a ripcord, making ambulance noises all the way through to the alley. I probably frightened the poor animal half to death.

Years later, I grew inordinately fond of a wonderful old boxer, Suki, who belonged to my landlady in Stratford-on-Avon, Peggie McDonald. While other actors swanned in and out of the Dirty Duck and swarmed the noticeboard for possible breakages among star limbs, night after night Peggie, Suki and I sat there three in a row, our suppers on our laps (well, Suki's lap left a lot to be desired but she made mincemeat of ours), and poured scorn on bad TV from sedentary heights. Suki had character. She was, if anything, rather grandiose, with an airy, often slightly pie-eyed look that suggested she might well have been at the cooking sherry while we were out. And I tell you, until you've been wakened in the wee small hours by a boxer's tongue all over your bare essentials, you haven't lived – and there'll be no Mike Tyson jokes at this juncture, thank you.

No, dog-wise, I think I Peked with Emily – the Brontë-named Yorkshire terrier and downstairs inhabitant of our first married flat. Emily decided to make us welcome in her own way. She chose, curiously enough, to do this at meal times. No sooner did the can-opener come out or the gas fail to ignite, than Emily would step out and start what we could only describe as her *Meandering Heights*. She would pad up the steps in a sort of jaunty, jowly way, glance round casually, sniffing the air, and then, as if an interesting new thought had occurred to her, she would stroll across the front of the window, pause – yet, it has to be said, nonchalantly – then swiftly mount our kitchen steps virtually whistling with indifference. It was a class act, followed by her look of absolute amazement when inevitably the contents of our plates found their way on to hers. Chaplin must have based a lot of *The Kid* on Emily.

The only pet to grace Schloss Rosenthal, save Zuckerman, the much-chronicled tortoise and escapologist, has been the tabby bought for Child One when Child Two came along to screw up her life. Pushkin and the aforementioned assassin are now seventeen years old and it's hard to say which of them is more eccentric. Pushkin sleeps, disastrously, on my head, wipes her nether regions on my script, waits by the garage for my car to return from the show, tells me when to brush her, lies cradled in my arms when I'm on my trampoline, and dismembers my tights.

She is fed, vetted and nursed by my husband and she only has eyes for me. Which is why I love her. Every fraction of upholstery in the house resembles Shredded Wheat, the chair legs are grated and I still love her.

She's slowing up and takes the stairs with stiff back legs. Sometimes she jumps optimistically on to the dressing table and misses. Sometimes her eyes look cloudy. I'll never tell her I've always wanted a dog, or that one day I may throw cat flaps to the wind and buy two beagles. At last then I'll be able to invite Mum over for Sunday morning Beagles and Licks.

CHRISTOPHER MATTHEW

Small Fry

o O o

For Proust's madeleine read Matthew's frogspawn. I was out in Richmond Park at the time, giving the dog an early spring airing, when I happened to look down into this stream and there it was, sloshing about amongst the weeds, looking like half a pound of undercooked tapioca. For a moment or two I couldn't make out what it was, and then I felt a jolt of recognition, not dissimilar to the sort one gets on spotting an old girl friend across a crowded room. The soft-focus lens was pulled, the Elgar welled up on the soundtrack and suddenly I was a small boy again, kneeling beside the stream at the bottom of the field behind our house in Oxted, aertex-ed arm plunged into the freezing water, scooping up spawn by the Kilnerful.

I can't pretend that I ever harboured very strong feelings for the little army of tadpoles which emerged in the warm sunlight on the kitchen windowsill. I don't suppose they were that mad about me either – staring at them all the time like that. On the other hand, they didn't exactly disrupt the daily round. Unlike the dachshund and the grey Persian, they didn't get under my mother's feet in the kitchen, or hang about waiting for food, or dig holes in the herbaceous border. In fact they didn't do anything very much, though they did have this trick of floating at attention for minutes on end without moving, which provided hours of mindless entertainment that Chris Evans and the Big Breakfast brigade would kill for.

The other enormous advantage tadpoles had over cats, dogs, hamsters and the like was that the moment they showed signs of amphibiosity and generally getting above themselves, you simply took them back where they came from. And tadpole-bonding being very much in its infancy, there was rarely a wet eye in the house – though, of course, I cannot speak for the tadpoles.

Obviously the tadpole cannot hold a candle to the kind of pet that marks a child out as a budding Durrell and Attenborough,the grass snake, the gecko and the praying mantis, not least because tadpoles do not take kindly to being carried round in the pockets of small boys' grey flannel shorts. On the other hand, as a child of the forties, one rubbed shoulders with nature on a pretty regular basis, and looking down at that gobbet of speckled spawn in that stream in Richmond, I couldn't help feeling a twinge of regret that my own sons have reached the ages of 14 and 12 without experiencing the simple pleasures of the jam jar. Ditto that I didn't happen to have one on me at the time.

But Dame Nature can always be relied on to have a surprise or two up her sleeve, and a few days later, what should I spy, struggling across the lawn, but a brown furry caterpillar. In my day, chances are it would have had a brightly coloured tuft on its head, like a feather on a grand vizier's turban, but standards have slipped in the caterpillar world along with everything else, and besides, it's an established entomological fact – as documented in my *Wonder Book of Creepy-Crawlies* – that the duller the caterpillar, the more brilliant the butterfly. So I duly jam-jarred the creature, along with a handful of grass and a couple of small lettuce leaves, covered it with a piece of cling-film, punched a few holes in it, and shoved it up on the kitchen shelf.

Suddenly, it was sun-burst sandal time all over again. If the voices of Nature Parliament had suddenly come winging out of the wireless and my wife had appeared in the doorway with a jar of Bemax, I would not have been surprised. Unfortunately, my children did not enter into the spirit of the proceedings with quite the enthusiasm I had hoped for. Neither did the caterpillar. I don't think I've ever seen an insect looking so down-in-the-mouth. William said perhaps it didn't care for the food. I said I'd never heard such nonsense in my life. If a furry brown had turned up its nose at a good English lettuce in my day, it would have felt the rough side of my tongue. What on earth did they imagine caterpillars lived on if it wasn't lettuce leaves?

'Mangetout?' said Nicholas.

William suggested it might be feeling homesick, so I rigged up a small twig for it to climb up, but if I'd bought it a Super-Nintendo it couldn't have been less interested.

'Never mind,' I said. 'Just think. One of these days, it'll turn into a Red Admiral, or a Dorset Blue.'

'A corpse, more likely,' said Nicholas.

The following morning they came rushing in with the astonishing news that there were now two caterpillars in the jar. It was some time before we realised that what we were staring at was not a new-born baby but dead skin. I said that I couldn't remember any caterpillar of mine sloughing its skin.

Nicholas said, 'You couldn't remember the imperfect subjunctive of *duco* either.'

Meanwhile, the caterpillar had got its appetite back in no uncertain terms and was attacking the lettuce like a junkie on a fresh line of coke. William said he thought it had grown. I told him he was imagining things.

We came in that evening to find the blooming thing had done a runner. Typical. That's the last time I give a caterpillar its own climbing frame. We turned the kitchen upside down but we never found it. I reckon it's still there somewhere, lurking behind the fridge, biding its time. Any day now my wife's going to walk in and be confronted by some mutated monster, looking like Jeff Goldblum in *The Fly*, dripping acid all over the working surfaces and frightening the dog. And before we know what, the SAS will be abseiling down the side of the house, and half Harwell will be in here blasting the thing to smithereens with ray guns, and the kitchen will need redecorating, and we'll find we're not fully insured, and three guesses who'll get the blame?

But then, of course, as I keep reminding the children, life was so much more straightforward when I was a boy.

ALAN PLATER

The Wild Pigs of Thorngumbald

o ◯ o

Once upon a time in another country called the late fifties, I had a job in an architects' office. It lasted for eighteen months, before I set aside grown-up things and became a full-time writer.

Our drawing office was a Dickensian attic in Scale Lane, in the heart of Hull's medieval Old Town, almost opposite Charlie Foster's legendary sandwich shop. The work-force – maximum half-a-dozen – was flexible, nomadic and given to quiet anarchy. Most of them were running small private practices on the side, using the boss's time and tracing paper. I was the exception, fully occupied not finishing a comic novel. The boss was a gentle, innocent man called Brian, who had inherited the firm and probably deserved better.

Lunch comprised one of Charlie Foster's cheese-and-pickle sandwiches and thirty-two games of darts, 301 up, start and finish on a double, with our resident quantity surveyor, Eric, a gold-mine of rude jokes and one-liners.

'What's the difference between a war-horse and a cart-horse?'

'I don't know, Eric, what *is* the difference between a war-horse and a cart-horse?'

'A war-horse darts into the fray.'

Had it not been for the darts, I might have finished the novel. Score one for the dartboard.

The dialogue was sharp, and distorted my dramatic style for ever. The office was something of a social centre, especially in working hours. Displacement activity was a high art form. Our senior draughtsman's son wandered in one day to tell us about his new girl friend. The lad was an occasional skiffle player and therefore a bit of a dude by local standards.

'She's wonderful,' he said. 'We go dancing every night.'

'Ballroom?'

'Can't complain.'

Bernard, our office junior, was an amiable young man who went to Charlie's for the sandwiches and the cigarettes, ran off the prints, fell in love regularly and knew all the words to 'Great Balls Of Fire'. Like me, he was supposed to go to day-release lectures at a local college. He never went. Nor did I. Sometimes we didn't go together, usually because there was an important field to be measured.

Fields were our speciality. All over the East Riding of Yorkshire there are housing estates, crammed tight with developments best described as bungaloid: a word coined, I think, by the late Ian Nairn. Bernard and I started the process with our semi-dedicated measuring.

The challenge was to cram as many houses or bungalows into the field as ingenuity, and occasional perjury, would allow. Architects were paid on a royalty principle: so much for the basic design and a smaller sum each time that design was repeated within the given field. Therefore the greater the density of bungaloid, the greater the income. Karl Marx and Adam Smith wrote extensively on this theme.

Our finest adventure was in a field close to a village called Thorngumbald on the plain of Holderness to the east of the city: Larkin country. The word is pronounced more or less as written though I recall Hull people calling it: 'Thorninghambald'. Supplementary syllables were never compulsory. Brandesburton, for example, was generally called 'Bott'n'. In the matter of spoken English, Hull and the East Riding are a rich and perverse province.

The Thorngumbald field was irregular, as fields are wont to be: a bit cheese-shaped, as Brian used to say. We had ways of getting the answers right, or of fudging them if we forgot to check a vital dimension on the day. The single inescapable necessity was to measure the boundaries of the site. This we did with a linen tape, a hundred feet long. Bernard held one end and I held the other. We repeated the process until all the essential dimensions had been checked; and double-checked, if it was a nice day.

We had noticed the pigs when we entered the field. They were in a corner, grazing or chewing their cud or reflecting on the rapidly changing nature of their universe or whatever the hell pigs did in those days. We were city-dwellers, young, urbane and sophisticated. What did we care? Had we been in a mid-nineties television drama series, our dialogue would have run:

'Measuring fields. It's our job. It's what we do.'

I was holding one end of the tape against a legally significant post marking the corner of the field and Bernard was holding the other end, buried deep in a hedge.

'Stop pulling so tight,' I said, abandoning grammar in the pursuit of professionalism.

'I'm not,' he said.

We turned to see the tape had been attacked by the pigs. They had seized upon it and were strung out along it, chewing it with expressions that were tricky to interpret. Happiness? Hunger? Revolution?

Phrases flashed into my mind: string of pearls? string of swine? There was a one-liner hiding somewhere. Bernard, ever the more practical, said: 'What are we going to do?'

Fortunately, I had done vacation work on a farm at a time when agriculture was still labour-intensive. I had worked with pigs and had been advised by an experienced farm labourer how to deal with them.

'If they get funny, kick the sods on the nose. They don't like it. Well, would you?'

Ideologically speaking, what happened next was pretty

unsound, but truth is sacred, or so it says on Life's Wrapper and my Writers' Guild union card. We retrieved the tape by a mixture of frenzied yelling and unsubtle footwork. There was no attempt to explain to the pigs, patiently and rationally, our side of the problem, or to understand theirs.

We caught the next bus back to Hull. In the fifties there were buses, yea even unto places like Thorngumbald, and people used them. Back at the office, Brian said:

'Did you finish the survey?'

'Not quite.'

'Well why did you come back?'

'The tape got chewed by pigs.'

We showed him the tape by way of evidence.

The only other animal incident I remember was when Bernard fell in love with the girl he eventually married and announced that he was going to buy her a dog for Christmas.

'Don't do it,' said Eric.

'Why not?'

'They're a bugger to wrap up.'

ANDREW LLOYD WEBBER

Semper Felix

o ◯ o

My mother, Jean died of cancer late last year. She was mental about cats to the point of total obsession. When my brother Julian and I had to clear up her flat, we not only had to find a home for her beloved two blue Burmese, but also for a library of cat books which filled a small van.

I owe a lot to my mother, for among many things it was she who read me when I was very young, T S Eliot's *Old Possum's Book of Practical Cats*. It was one of those memories that stuck and of course it was, forgive this, the catalyst to my musical based on that brilliant, cheeky set of 'off-duty' Eliot poems. Minor Eliot, some would say, but I would argue among the best lyrics any composer has had the luck to work with, for lyrics they are.

However, there were various inconsistencies about Mummy's passion for cats. First, she had bad asthma. She blamed this on time spent listening to my father playing the organ at All Saints, Margaret Street. But she was not complaining about my father. The asthma was, she alleged, the consequence of the incense liberally used in this, the most admirable temple of Anglo-Catholicism.

I used to think aged ten or thereabouts it all very curious, because my father had resigned from All Saints, Margaret Street, just after I was born. 'Could it be our cats that are giving you asthma?' I would suggest. 'Nonsense, darling,' she would say, 'my Perseus doesn't give me asthma, it was all those dreadful priests who preached that a cat has no soul.'

I suppose the musical *Cats* is all about cats most definitely having a soul. T S Eliot himself was an Anglo-Catholic and many of the ideas we incorporated are about his beliefs, although I have no idea whether his religious views embraced the teachings at All Saints, Margaret Street that apparently gave my mother this asthma.

All I do know is that Eliot loved dogs as much. His widow Valerie explained to me why Pollicle Dogs are Pollicle Dogs, and Jellicle Cats are Jellicle Cats. It was his private joke about English upper-crust accents. Poor Little Dogs became Pollicle Dogs and Dear Little Cats, Jellicle Cats.

I am writing this in a break between working with Tom Stoppard on his screenplay of the proposed film of *Cats*. It will be animated, and a journey of exploration for me as I've never done anything like this before. But win, lose or draw, I have my mother to thank for this adventure and I hope that somewhere in the Heavyside Layer she lives in a world of cats, my father and no asthma.

ALAN COREN

Sea Change

o ◯ o

A public beach has been put out of bounds at Great Yarmouth so that fifty pairs of little terns can nest in peace. A stretch of shore a third of a mile long and a hundred yards wide has been cleaned and roped off.

The terns have flown 4,000 miles from Gambia to mate.

Daily Telegraph

'I can remember when you couldn't get on that beach without a tie,' said the crab, from the edge of the rock-pool.

The gull, perched on the ledge above it, glanced down.

'Must have been a bugger to knot,' it observed, 'with claws.'

One stalked eye emerged slowly from the crab's armoured slot and stared at the gull for a time.

'What?' it said.

'Bow tie, was it?' enquired a prawn, breaking the surface. 'I couldn't help hearing.'

'It would have to be,' said the gull. 'He could hardly wear the other sort.'

'I've always wondered what they were called,' said the prawn, thoughtfully. 'Has it ever struck you as funny, having one called a bow and the other one not called anything?'

'No, it hasn't,' said the gull.

The crab's other eye came out.

'Why would he have to wear a bow, anyway?' asked the prawn.

'First off,' said the gull, 'it would go better with his shape. But mainly, it's the practical side. If he wore the other kind of tie, it would trail in the mud.'

'It would be filthy,' nodded the prawn, 'in no time. I see that.'

'Plus trip him up. It is one of the shortcomings of running side-ways. The tie would hang down in front,' explained the gull, 'and he would be forever running over it.'

'Unless he had the knot on one side,' said the prawn.

'He'd look ridiculous,' said the gull.

The prawn considered this.

'Beats me why they wanted him to wear a tie at all,' it said.

'They were probably partial,' murmured a winkle who had hitherto kept itself to itself, 'to a nice bit of dressed crab!'

At which it convulsed so uncontrollably as to lose its grip on the underside of the rock, drop to the sand, and roll about, hoot-ing.

'*Nice bit of dressed crab!*' it shrieked. 'Where do I get 'em from!'

The gull rose on a single flap, sank smartly to the beach, and put a yellow claw on the winkle.

'Shall I do us all a favour?' it enquired.

'Leave it out,' said the winkle, muffled. 'It is not as if I can help myself. It is in the blood, if you are a winkle. Generations of salty Cockney wit etcetera. It is expected of us. Also, being cheery goes with ending up on a pin. Look at the First World War. *Nil carborundum* and so forth. Gassed last night, and gassed the night before. *Are we downhearted?* No!'

'Oh, let him go,' said the crab, wearily. 'It is the oldest joke in the book.'

'*I* laughed,' said the prawn.

'It's the way I tell 'em,' said the winkle.

The gull resumed its perch.

'I still don't understand,' it said, 'where they expected you to get a tie from.'

The crab sighed. Bubbles winked on its terrible jaws.

'Not *me*,' it said. 'They did not expect *me* to wear a tie. They expected one another to wear 'em. The men wore sponge-bag trousers and striped blazers and Panama hats, and the women wore long frocks and bonnets with daisies on, it was all very elegant, this beach.'

'Pull this one,' said the prawn, 'they would have gone down like bricks.'

'They did not wear 'em in the water,' said the crab, rolling each eye independently. 'Don't you know anything? When they wanted to swim, they went inside those little hut efforts, and they changed into bathing suits, and someone pushed the huts into the water, and they got out of the back door and into the sea.'

'Stone me!' cried the prawn. 'What a palaver! It's not even as if they eat plankton. They just go in and lollop about a bit and then they come out and turn red. Fancy going to the expense of a hut!'

The crab sighed.

'You had to be there,' it murmured. 'It had a lot of charm. It had innocence. They used to bring ukuleles and butterfly nets. They used to play French cricket and sing 'My Old Man Said Follow the Van'. They did not,' muttered the crab darkly, 'have nude beaches. They did not,' and here he waved a gnarled claw towards the roped enclosure, 'have subsidised mating.'

'Oh, look!' cried the winkle, as the others, on the crab's signal, stared.

'What is it?' said the gull.

'She's having one of her terns!' shrieked the winkle.

The prawn fell about.

'You may laugh,' said the crab, 'but it is not only a gross affront to decency, it is a wanton misuse of council money. Little terns coming over here, having it away on the rates.'

'I wonder why we never see any great terns,' said the gull.

'He's right, you know,' said the winkle. 'Remember Jimmy James? Jewell and Warriss? Remember Wilson, Keppel and Betty? They all played here once. I blame television.'

'*Great turns!*' howled the prawn, clutching itself octapodally. 'You are a caution, and no mistake! Have you ever thought of doing it professionally yourself?'

The winkle shook its shell.

'It's a terrible life, these days,' it replied. 'All they want is smut. Or impressions of Robin Day. Not easy, if you happen to be a mollusc. Besides, very few of 'em speak winkle.'

'It would not surprise me,' said the crab, 'if there was not a ban on tern jokes. They have, after all, flown here from Gambia. It would not surprise me if making tern jokes was punishable under the Race Relations Act.'

'I wonder why they don't do it at home?' enquired the gull. 'Fancy flying halfway round the world for a bit of wing-over! I usually manage with a lump of driftwood. It's a bad day for me if I have to go further than fifty feet.'

'They come over here,' replied the crab bitterly, 'on account of it is the life of Riley. Roped-off beach, no cats, no tar, no donkey doings, RSPB patrols, nothing to do all day except –'

'– take terns!' said the winkle. 'Sorry, sorry, slipped out!'

'In all probability,' said the gull, 'they do not even have to build anything. They probably get a council nest. They probably go straight to the top of the list. Fly in, make your clawprint in the space provided, ten minutes later you are –'

'– going for a quick tern along the beach!'

'I'd write all these down,' spluttered the prawn, 'if the tide wasn't coming in.'

'It would not surprise me,' muttered the gull, 'if they did not even have to be married. It is probably an offence to ask 'em. You know councils. Give 'em half a chance to be seen doing sunnink for the single-parent egg, and before you know it they are coming round with a red-checked tablecloth and a candle in a bottle and a hot lugworm dinner with all the trimmings.'

'They look after their own, all right,' muttered the crab. 'Bloody clever, these Communists.'

'Sharp left terns,' said the winkle.

The prawn fell back, waving its pleopods feebly.

'Lucky I haven't got ribs,' it wheezed, 'I'd be strapped up by now!'

'They just come to me,' explained the winkle. 'Call it a gift.'

'You could've made a fortune in saucy postcards,' said the prawn warmly, when it had recovered, 'with the right contacts.'

'I've never understood why they're supposed to be saucy,' said the winkle. 'They're usually about the ones with hair under their noses asking the ones with two lumps on the front if they would care for a nice big winkle. What's so saucy about that?'

'Not just Communists, either,' said the gull, darkly. 'A fair number of 'em are gay. That is what attracts councils more than anything, these days.'

'There's a big ternover,' said the winkle.

'Is there no end to his repertoire?' cried the prawn.

'Bottomless,' replied the winkle.

They both fell over.

'I can remember,' said the crab, 'when what councils spent their money on was deckchairs and bandstands and lifebelts and little lights on the lamp-posts and stopping piers from rotting and men going round with spikes picking rubbish up off the sand. What is it all coming to?'

'It is probably a symbol of something,' said the gull. 'A lot of things are, these days.'

'Where will it all end?' asked the prawn.

'In moral depravity, is where,' said the crab.

'Tern to page three,' said the winkle.

RAY CONNOLLY

Black and White and Led All Over

o ◯ o

He was the most genuine gift I ever received. And for sixteen years there has scarcely been a day I have not shared with him. Even now as I write he sits on my mantelpiece, black ears and button eyes, his stubby arms still out, forlornly awaiting the embrace which now rarely comes.

In our travelling days we must, I can see, have made an odd couple, trekking together across continents, custom halls and hotel lobbies, me a grown man, him an old, stuffed panda, pushed untidily into my hand baggage, as often as not with one leg poking out.

He could have travelled in my suitcase: he would hardly have complained. But that would have been to shut him off and cut the link he represented. That would have been to deny the point. He had been given to me as a companion and a replacement, as a comfort and reminder. He was then and he is now.

He belonged originally to my son Kieron, given as a Christmas present in 1974 when Kieron was one. He was an instant success and, as soon Kieron would hardly venture outside the house without him, Panda took to travelling early in life.

In 1977 our whole family went to New Zealand by way of Los Angeles, and there on every single snapshot is Panda: tucked as reassurance under Kieron's arm, outfacing Mickey and Goofy in Disneyland, gazing unmoved at the dead shark strung up in the Bay of Islands, wide-awake in the jumbo jet as the sun rose over the Pacific and the sleeping children.

Sometimes Panda wore a patch over one eye, because in those days, between eye operations, Kieron wore a patch. Sometimes he refused, because sometimes Kieron refused. We were a family of six: Plum and I, then Louise, Dominic and Kieron, and Panda.

Then when Kieron was six and off skiing, for just about the one and only time a new panda appeared in his Avoriaz bunk at night, a satin-coated charmer, a cleaner, softer fellow. How fickle children can be in their affections, I mused to myself, as the new companion replaced the old. But I may have been mistaken. To Kieron they were probably simply different manifestations of the same thing.

The following summer I stayed behind in London to work while Plum and the children went to Cornwall for a holiday. 'What will I do when you leave me?' I said to Kieron, who at six, was earnestly packing his little bag. 'Who will I cuddle then?'

He didn't answer. But he must have thought about it. That night as I climbed into bed there was someone waiting for me. The old, recently neglected Panda was lying on my pillow, tucked under the sheets. I would have someone to cuddle after all.

No one prompted Kieron. It was a spontaneously thoughtful act by a little boy. Panda was all he had to give me.

When we get older and begin to know about these things I suspect we give in order to receive. We buy love. But Kieron was too young to know about that.

Panda had been Kieron's and now he was mine. And he still is. But, as an animal might become a totem for a whole tribe, Panda quickly came to represent not just Kieron but my home and family, all three of my children.

From that day Panda often slept with me when the family were away. When they were at home he joined me in my study. I never travelled without him. I'm not a superstitious person, but it would have seemed an act of betrayal to leave him behind, to be tempting something terrible to happen in my absence.

Consequently Panda has known many strange hotel bedrooms, he and I being viewed with amusement, not to say suspicion, by chambermaids from Rio de Janeiro to Bombay.

It was our Las Vegas adventure that caused the greatest consternation. We were staying in Caesar's Palace Hotel, billeted in a suite with a sunken bath, a mauve carpet, raspberry curtains and a saffron-coloured fourposter bed, in the canopy of which was hung a large mirror. The only thing missing, I suppose, was a host of nubile virgins – but then this was Las Vegas.

To be honest it wasn't exactly our sort of place. And marooned in that neon-glazed desert as we awaited the call of the appalling singer-actress who had summoned us, Panda and I found ourselves with considerable time to kill.

The devil finds work for idle hands. The overhead mirror intrigued me. This would be something for the children, I thought. An aerial photograph of Panda and me in Vegas.

Having just returned from the pool I was wearing my swimming shorts. Stretching out I lay Panda next to me and, prefocusing my camera, pressed the button with my outstretched finger. Very good. Next another angle, then another as I moved Panda around the bed: the two of us nose to nose, Panda lying on my chest, snuggling under my arm, sitting on my underpants; all kinds of positions. I really was very bored.

When we eventually got home I sent all the films of our latest travels off to the Iranian photo shop down the road. They were ready the next day, but something was missing. The frames showing Panda and me in Las Vegas had not been printed.

Perhaps I shouldn't have been surprised. The previous summer the same developers had refused to print shots of Plum's bare breasts. Now it was Panda's turn to be censored.

I never had the nerve to ask them what they thought had been going on in Las Vegas. If the Ayatollah wasn't keen on lady's bosoms, only Allah knew what he and they would think about a middle-aged man cavorting almost naked on a bed with a stuffed panda.

I stopped taking Panda on my travels shortly after that. He had been prodded and poked and X-rayed too many times at airport security desks. His luck was running out. Before long some over-zealous customs official was certain to slit him open looking for drugs. Besides the children were growing up. They were the ones who were going away now.

Panda still has his job to do. Sitting up there watching me he is still the symbol of my family, dispersed though it is now becoming.

I won't be given a present like Panda again.

HARRY SECOMBE

The Dog That Wouldn't Lie Down

o O o

'We'll definitely have to get this dog trained,' I said to Myra. I was lying on my back on the kitchen floor as I spoke, having been knocked flat for the umpteenth time by the Boxer which was now licking my face by way of apology.

'One of you will have to be trained,' said Myra dryly. 'You spoil that dog.'

I had to agree. Jimmy, as he was called, had wheedled his way into my heart as a puppy and though he was now the size of a small pony I had been letting him get away with murder. 'Discipline, that's what he wants,' I said grimly, trying to prevent him having an affair with my left leg.

Thus it was that a week later found us driving into the yard of a dog-training establishment in Sussex. We had found the address and telephone number in the Yellow Pages and after being assured that Jimmy would be well cared for during his three-week stay, we had decided to take him along.

He had been his usual ebullient self on the journey, licking the back of my neck as I drove and barking at every cat we passed.

He loved being taken for a ride and would jump in any vehicle parked in our driveway which happened to be left unattended with a door open. As much as he loved a drive, he hated men in uniform. Once he occupied a milk float for half-an-hour, baring his teeth at the terrified milkman everytime he approached.

'Perhaps if you took your Unigate hat off he might let you get in,' said my practical wife, who had just arrived on the scene. He did and Jimmy immediately let him get aboard. We picked him up at the depot at the end of the milkman's shift.

Now, as we entered the kennels he looked around suspiciously. It began to dawn on him that he was about to be left behind here. He started to howl.

The owner of the establishment came out of his office and waved to us. He was an upright middle-aged man of military bearing and a brusque manner who liked to be called Major. Myra and I left the car and made ourselves known. In the back seat Jimmy kept up his howling, the rest of the kennels' inhabitants providing an accompaniment. It was like Woodstock with tails.

'Dont't worry about his howling,' said the major. 'We'll soon cure him of that.' It crossed my mind that he didn't seem to have cured the other dogs of the problem.

He called a passing kennel maid and after some coaxing she got Jimmy to leave the car. He gave us a reproachful look as he was dragged around the corner on his lead.

'He'll be all right here. Just phone us once a week and we'll tell you how he's getting on.' The major was very firm.

We said our goodbyes and as we left the yard Jimmy flashed past with a distraught kennel maid in pursuit. 'Go on. Go on. We can handle him.' There was a touch of asperity in the major's voice.

'He'll be eating at the table with us when he comes back. Probably have his own knife and fork,' I said. This drew a slow secret smile from Myra. 'We'll see,' she replied.

We phoned at the end of the first week as the major had requested. 'Jimmy? Yes, well we haven't put him with the rest of the dogs yet. He's quite a character isn't he? Don't worry about him.'

It occurred to me that I was worrying at the rate of £30 a day.

When we called the following week there was a slight pause before the major replied. 'Is there any insanity in the family?'

'I had an aunt in Aberystwyth who went a bit peculiar,' I replied.

'No, no, man. In the dog's pedigree.'

'I've no idea.' I went and got the form we had received when we bought the dog. I read it out to him.

'Sounds all right,' the major said grudgingly.

'What's the matter with him?' I asked.

'Well, it's been snowing here and he refused to lie down in it. That set off the other dogs – they wouldn't lie down either.'

'I'd have thought that was rather sensible of him. After all there's not much hair on his belly. I haven't got much on mine and I certainly wouldn't do it.' My attempt at humour drew a groan from the other end of the line and the receiver was replaced with a bang.

Half way through the third week, the major rang us. 'Come and get your dog,' he said.

'What's he done?'

'I'll bloody tell you what he's done. He's got out and he's been chasing rabbits all over the countryside. Apart from that he's a bad influence on the other dogs.' There was a touch of hysteria in his voice. 'Come and take him away.' I think he had been crying.

We went and did just that. Jimmy was overjoyed to see us and licked the back of my neck all the way home.

There was no apparent change in his behaviour until one wet Saturday morning when I took him with me to the local photography shop. He was his usual boisterous self and I became embarrassed when he knocked over a pyramid of film cartons. The shop was crowded and the films rolled all over the floor.

'SIT!' I yelled. To my utter amazement, he sat right there and then in the middle of the shop surrounded by a kaleidoscope of Kodak colour film. There was a spatter of applause from the other customers. I acknowledged it with some pride.

I paid for my purchases and prepared to leave. 'Come on,' I said to Jimmy. He just sat and looked at me. Obviously I had not used the right word of command or the correct tone of voice. 'UP!' I cried. Nothing. 'On your feet.'

Jimmy's naturally furrowed brow furrowed even further. You could see that he was trying hard to remember the code word, but he remained firmly locked in the sitting position. The other customers were sniggering now, their approval of my former mastery forgotten.

I tried leaving the shop, hoping he'd follow. Instead he started to howl. There was only one thing for it. I picked him up and carried him out of the shop and all the way home while the rain poured down relentlessly.

When Myra opened the door she regarded us both with some amusement. 'Put him down,' she said. That was the word that unlocked Jimmy from his paralysis. 'DOWN!'

Typically, he had confused the command 'DOWN' for 'UP'. He leapt from my arms with a joyful bark and made straight for the cat.

'SIT!' shouted Myra, and he sat.

'Let's leave him there for a bit,' she said, heading for the kitchen. 'I'll put the kettle on.'

MICHAEL BYWATER

Outback of
Beyond

o O o

I am writing this sitting under a . . . no. It won't do. I *hate* people who say that. 'I am writing this . . . ?' Big shots. Smart-arses. Look-at-me, oh aren't I clever, actually *writing* this. Well, huh. Our ancestors chiselled their sacred religious texts onto the skulls of their enemies, and they are still as good a read as you'd find this side of a Jeffrey Archer novel; one thing you can say about Jeffrey Archer, he may not be an intellectual but he's a *bloody good storyteller*. Right? Yes.

To tell you the truth, I could just handle a nice Jeffrey Archer novel now. But I cannot have one. I am writing this (*pftui!*) sitting on my swag under the shade of a coolabah tree next to Cooper Creek in the middle of the Australian Outback. Near here, the explorers Burke and Wills met their deaths. I imagine they said: 'Hello, deaths. Boy, are we glad to see *you*,' and if that sounds cynical, you have clearly never sat under a coolabah tree in the middle of the Australian Outback, and probably believe that the word 'swag' is flanked by the words 'jolly' and 'man',

107

whereas the appropriate words should be 'miserable' and 'fly-food'.

Before I came out here to write about flying around the Outback in a little aeroplane, I saw the place in strictly *National Geographic* terms. 'Silhouetted against the setting sun', I thought to myself, 'the immemorial aboriginal murmurs his ancestral myths, lost in the legends of the ancient Dreamtime'. Sometimes the part of my brain which wanted me to go on this trip would send up headlines: *Red Dust and Cold Beer in Australia's Heartlands.*

But the truth was different, as it always is. There is enough red dust to set up a business, particularly after I had taxied my ageing Cessna 182 down the main dirt street of Innamincka Township (one pub, one store and any number of sweating old-age pensioners tootling madly across the desert in their air-conditioned 4WDs, and whatever happened to those dear, dead days when OAPs would sit on the step, gawping?) but you may look in vain for silence. My own personal coolabah tree (named after a brand of cheap white wine which TV commercials encourage us not to sell to aboriginals) is teeming and fecund with a hideous diversity of brute creation, red in tooth and claw – and indeed in everything else, thanks to the dust – and all of it shouting its head off. There are galahs, an elegant parrot with a rose madder breast: their name has become Australian slang for irritating stupidity, something you could understand if you'd been woken up each morning by their mad yelling as they flew about and crashed into each other.

There are crows; but they are not our atmospheric British crows who caw occasionally at dusk across the cool, mist-haunted fields. These crows are lacking in discretion. They caw all day long, and far into the night. I suspect they are drunk, because anything can set them off. At dawn they caw because the sun has come up. During the day they caw with hideous, pissed exuberance because – hey –it's daytime and – hey! – the *sun* is *shining*. At sunset they caw because – Oi! – something's happening to the sun! What can it be? Help! Oi! And for most of the night they caw because it's dark and spooky and – wow! – there might be *anything* out there, who can tell?

Nor is it even a decent, British, fog-bound smoker's caw. The caw of the black outback crow is plaintive, anguished and melismatic. It is the caw of a crow who, in the grip of *delirium tremens*, is no longer sure of what's what, except that the world is bad, life is hard, and its mother didn't love it. It sounds, so far as it sound like anything on earth, like a Siamese cat on heat. When I first heard it, I though it *was* a Siamese cat on heat, but the question of why it was flying back and forth above my head seemed fairly insignificant because of the Nice Cold Beer. But hearing randy flying cats when drunk is one thing, and hearing them in the morning when all too painfully sober is another. It can be perplexing until you learn the Australian way of dealing with such natural phenomena of the animal kingdom, which is:

1 Get drunk.
2 Stay drunk.

By adopting this simple two-stage plan, it is possible to cope with the Australian fauna. There are things out here which are perfectly acceptable as long as you can believe they are merely the tortured figments of a disordered mind, but which, if you suspected they were real, could cause you to lose your senses. The first man to see a kangaroo must have thought that it was simply a question of too much *pituri* at the *corra borra*, and he'd be all right in the morning. When it was still there the next day, and everyone else said, yes, they'd seen it too, and they figured it was just something they'd have to live with, you can see that there was nothing for it but to wander aimlessly about the country, inventing improbable ancestral myths and hoping against hope that one day you'd hit on a spot where you never again had to see anything quite so unforgivably *weird*.

And then the white men came, and it all started again. Since we already had as fine a set of improbable ancestral myths as you could shake a stick at, we had to come up with something else, and the something else was the bullet. We shot kangaroos and ate their tails. We shot the loud-mouthed pigeons and stewed them over the camp fire (NB, says my nineteenth-century bush cooking book, 'this dish can equally be made with parrots or budgerigars.') We shot snakes, just for the hell of it ('Dreadful tucker,'

109

says my book, 'fit only for blackfellas,' while another book tells me the aboriginals viewed with disgust the white men's alleged habit of eating 'unclean food, like snakes'.) We even shot Tasmanians, since Tasmania was known to be uninhabited and therefore they must be that *really* horrible freak of nature: animals that looked exactly like human beings. Shoot them! Now.

But still – with the exception of the poor Tasmanians – the animal kingdom triumphed. Kangaroos and huge, goofy emus make the northward track up through Broken Hill, a hazard to the peripatetic oldsters in their Toyota Land Cruisers. Dingos still hang around the town at night, fossicking in the pub yard. You still have to shake out your clothes each morning, a ritual attended by all sorts of scamperings, slitherings and gibberings, as well as the occasional fierce and furtive bit. Rabbit-proof fences hundreds of miles long have failed to solve the rabbit problem since, when the fences were built, there were rabbits on both sides of it. The hapless koala, locked in its evolutionary backwater, still makes a living from the eucalyptus tree, not on the grounds that it likes it, or even that it's good at digesting it (which it is not) but simply because there's nothing else around that is prepared to touch it.

And above all others, the flies triumph. Sticky clouds of black flies which penetrate the hat-net, come through windows and down chimneys, and cluster round every living thing in a horrible, malignant swarm. I am sitting on my swag under a coolabah tree down by Cooper Creek and the flies are so thick around my head that I can hardly see the screen. Fortunately, my little laptop computer has a very limited battery life, and in a moment the screen will dim; then I can stop being intrepid and head for the pub. Get drunk; stay drunk. The animal kingdom can fend for itself, and seems to be doing a good job of it, out here in the dead heart of Australia, where nothing can possibly live.

HUNTER DAVIES

Shellsuited

o O o

When Caitlin was aged 8 and Jake was 6 we were driving north to visit the grandparents and round about Spaghetti Junction we told them something exciting was going to happen, there's going to be a big surprise in our family pretty soon, can you guess?

'We're having a kitten,' said Caitlin.

'We're getting a puppy,' said Jake.

I should really have let them out there and then, find their own way up the M6 to Carlisle. All I said was wash your mouth out. Never, never let me hear such disgusting thoughts again.

The big news was that we were going to have another little human being, who turned out to be Flora, our little flower. Trust them to spoil it by wittering on about bleedin animals.

I thought I'd made it clear the moment they arrived, fresh out of the womb, or the cabbage patch or wherever, I wasn't there at the time, gone for a pie, hadn't I, that they were now entering an Animal Free Zone. No cats, dogs, ponies, rabbits, fish, gerbils, birds, performing fleas, is that clear, right, sign here, otherwise you're going straight back in the cabbage.

Why were we so horrid, you ask? What made us so anti-animal? My dear wife comes from an animal-free house, so that might have been one element. In my house we did at one time have a pet, a cat called Peter with three legs. It didn't always have three legs. It disappeared while we were living in Dumfries, not seen for weeks, not even a postcard, presumed dead, then it reappeared in the middle of one night, dragging a trap behind it. The vet cut off the damaged foot, leaving a nasty stump, and Peter lived happily ever after. But we didn't. At night, you would hear it going round the house – pad, pad, pad, THUMP; pad, pad, pad, THUMP. It reminded me of horrible stories by Wilkie Collins, creepy tales by R L wassisname, all of which I hadn't read at the time, nor since, come to think of it.

We like to think we were pro-humans, not anti-animal. Kids are hard enough to bring up anyway, all that snot, all that mess, all that noise, and that's just teenagers, without having to worry about their pets. We'd come from a long line of families which had babies, in fact having babies goes back, oh I dunno, must be generations, so you pick up, if just by Os Mosis, always loved his music, how to look after babies. But if you come from an animal-free home, it's all mystery. What does ON HEAT mean, for example? How do you neuter a goldfish? Most worrying of all, what do you do with the bloody things when you go off on holiday abroad? So, we decided to have none of them.

Ah, but having pets makes children caring, gives them a sense of responsibility. What cobblers! Let them love each other. Or me. I need caring for, don't I? My food put out, taken for a walk, cuddled, patted, my hair brushed. Can't expect my dear wife to do everything for me on her own.

All three children have now left home, tra la. One of them, dear Caitlin, has gone animal mad. The last time we saw her she had four stupid, horrible, nasty smelly dogs, all crawling all over her house, yuck. She's married and lives in Botswana, Africa, in the back of beyond, where there's not a lot of diversion, so I suppose playing with these dopey animals keeps her off the desert. She does have lots of space. The other two live in London flats, so no room for pets, but I don't think they'll succumb. With a bit of luck we've brainwashed them.

So, that just leaves the three of us at home. Yes, three. Didn't I mention we have a pet? Oh yes. Just before they all left home, we got a pet. We were only against the kids having them. No one said we couldn't have one. Whose house is it anyway.

My criteria for having an animal are very simple: it must be able to feed itself, water itself, amuse itself, make no noise, cause no trouble, no mess, not mind us going away for months on end and stay outside all year long. Can you guess what it is? No, this is not a trick. It's a real live animal, whom we love dearly. Its name is Tortee. Not a very original name for a tortoise. But I do love her dearly. Or him. We did try to sex her or him by turning it upside down and looking at its bum, sorry shell. Convex means it's a women, and concave a man. Or the opposite. That's what we couldn't remember, hence the name Tortee, which gives nothing away about its sexual preference.

The first year we had it, we put it to sleep in a box full of straw in the garage for winter, as instructed, and low and behold, Tortee woke up in the spring. Come the next autumn, we couldn't find her – I think she is a she – and we thought oh no, we've lost her. But in the spring, she reappeared, on her own, from some secret hideout. Since then, we've let her organise her own hibernation habits. I do think tortoises need privacy.

Nor do we feed her. Well, to amuse ourselves in the summer we might give her squashy strawberries or peaches, as she does have a sweet tooth, but there's no need to. My wife oils her shell once a year, but there again, that's for our aesthetic pleasure, so we can admire the grain, enjoy the texture, turn her into a talking point at garden parties. I'm sure Tortee doesn't give a tinkers.

I stroke her nose when I'm really bored, which is a weird sensation. The neck of a tortoise is very like the male member. Have you noticed? Actually, I don't want to go into this too closely. What happens between me and my tortoise is none of your business. We'll move on.

She can bite. DANGER – WILD TORTOISE: I put that on the garden gate once, to warn the next door's kids. If you try to stroke her neck too quickly, without the requisite foreplay, she can snap her jaws on your finger and draw blood. But not with me. I'm her best friend. It's probably the most exciting, surprising event in our family. Well, since Flora was born.

MATTHEW PARRIS

Dead
Bats

o O o

If scientists wish to investigate the human body's defences against stomach upset, I offer my own findings for their research. These days, I never, simply never, get an upset stomach. For the last year my alimentary canal has been proof against the most appalling assaults. More than a month in Peru and Bolivia, followed by a week in Albania, followed by the ultimate test, the Labour party conference in Blackpool, saw me sail confidently through digestive storms that reduced comrades to hunched, quivering wrecks.

What is my secret?

Well, now I think I know.

Let us start at the beginning. The water supply at my house in Derbyshire comes from a spring in the hillside. It pours into a stone trough and is then pumped up to a small storage tank in my loft.

The water is uncommonly pure and I do not treat it. I just drink it.

But for the last year or so, I have noticed a slight – very slight

– 'taste' to the water. Nothing to complain of, but you can tell; it makes the tea taste different. I thought little of it, though, until last weekend.

Now the taste was unmistakable – that same taste, but stronger. It was *almost* unpleasant. There was a very faint smell to the water.

Still, I was too busy to do anything about it. I drank the water as usual, and washed a couple of machine-loads of sheets, which should see me through to the end of the year. By Sunday I must have drunk a few gallons of the stuff, and felt fine. But that taste really wasn't right.

So I decided to check, starting with the stone trough. Frogs sometimes get into this trough, but I take the view that if they are still swimming, that is a good sign. I unlocked the cover. No, no frogs, dead or alive; no slugs either.

I tried a glass, removing a lively waterboatman. Tasted fine. Bother. That meant the loft, and the ladder with missing rungs, and the torch with the flat battery. Up I went.

As my eyes adjusted to the dark, I realised that the cover was off the little storage tank, and remembered taking it off last year and never replacing it. Hm. I shone the feeble beam into the murky depths, and looked. Something horrible looked back at me.

It was a bat. A very big bat. A very big dead bat. A very big *long*-dead bat. Oh yes, my friends, this (as Mrs Thatcher would say) was an ex-bat; a late bat; a previous bat. This bat had gone to meet its maker. So long ago, in fact, had this bat gone to meet its maker that it was only just recognisable as a bat. You could have mistaken it for a bad case of mushroom soup. Except, that is, for the little, sodden, furry face, which now stared eyeless up at me in unspoken reproach.

And I had been *drinking* that, probably all year. I fished out the bat bits and descended, queasily, to begin flushing the tank.

But have I not found the answer to stomach problems? Is not putrefied bat the way to immunise yourself against internal upset? Was it not the homeopathic drip-drip of ever more con-centrated decaying bat that had, over the months, fortified my stomach against Peruvian bacteria and Blackpool toxin?

This, surely, is the way to guarantee the health of the water-drinking masses: pollute the water! Forget your chlorine and your fluoride; a dead bat in every loft tank in every home throughout the kingdom should be our environmental health officers' goal.

There is now a flat taste to the Derbyshire water. Water-with-a-hint-of-bat was what I had become used to. I miss it. And I shall not bother to wash those sheets again. On a warm night, if I bury my face in them, they remind me.

JOAN BAKEWELL

Beware of the Dog

o O o

I don't particularly like animals, which is why what I'm going to tell you is so strange. The particular events I shall relate might much more appropriately have happened to someone else. But in fact they happened to me. Some five years ago now. Why was I chosen? And if so, who did the choosing? I don't know much about animals. In fact I seek to avoid them. So, if you like animals, perhaps you will have an explanation that comes more readily to those who understand and sympathise with them. Most particularly with dogs. Indeed, most particularly with gold Labradors. Most specifically, though you don't know her, with our own dog Molly. But I'm already running ahead of myself. Let me go back to the beginning. Then, when I've told my tale you will see that I need your advice.

It all began in the bar of the Ring o' Bells, the small country pub some half-mile down the road from my own modest little cottage. I was one of the first in the gathering rush to flee the traffic and pollution of city life. I came out here some eight years ago now, and with a fax machine – quite a novelty outside

London in those days – and two phone lines, I quickly set myself up in the work I was trained to do, as editor of popular romantic fiction. My authors are all women, too, and familiarity with the twists and co-incidences of story-telling makes them susceptible to the intriguing nature of my own story. One of them even suggested she might use it in her next paperback. But I was firm. This story is not only true. It is mine and it has serious implications for my future.

This particular spring evening in the Ring 'o Bells had all the liveliness and good humour I rely on to relieve the loneliness of my working life. Some of the local farm workers were in, joshing each other in a boisterous male way. The quiet middle-aged couple who run the local garden centre were sitting by the open fire doing a crossword. A gaggle of young girls spilled in through the door exclaiming with pleasure at the cosy welcome of the Ring's brass and timber-beamed interior.

I was sitting in my usual corner of the bar, passing the occasional remark with Maggie but content to watch the mellow scene. I didn't notice its arrival but suddenly a young gold Labrador was sitting at my feet and licking my hand. Acting on instinct I pulled the hand away. But curtness with animals doesn't go down well in a country pub. So I gave it a tentative pat on the head. To my consternation it then fixed me with a look of such yearning and devotion that I was considerably discomforted. I repeated the tap on the head. 'Good dog,' I said awkwardly. Isn't that what you say to dogs? Another pat and I turned back to my drink. Within minutes I was conscious that the dog had now placed its paw on my knee and was actually stroking me. I smiled rather wanly and cast around the pub to see if I could identify the owner. There was a smattering of strangers in the pub that night but no one suggested themselves.

By now I could no longer pursue my lonely musing at the bar, for the reason that I was no longer alone. The dog had attached itself to me. And I could no longer avoid the steady, I could almost say loving, gaze of this creature. I smiled back and ventured to stroke its golden back.

'Taken to you, all right – instant devotion, I'd say,' Maggie's comment confirmed my feeling that some new bond of friendship was being thrust upon me. Imagine, then, how startled I was by the abrupt, even rude, eruption of the dog's owner onto the scene. 'Got dogs of your own, then, that you go seducing others?' I stumbled to make sense of the remark. 'No, I haven't and . . . I didn't . . . Your dog seems to have attached itself to me.'

'Molly, come here, girl. The lady doesn't like dogs.'

'Oh, no. I'm just not used to them.' The golden Labrador – Molly – stayed put, her chin now reaching into my lap. I stroked her again, for the first time letting some warmth of feeling transmit itself to the creature I was now able to observe was indeed of particular and classic beauty. A fan of tail responded with pleasure to my touch.

'Do you live near here, then?' The owner parked himself on the stool beside me and I gave him the appraising look my lady novelists are so adept at. Tall and wiry, he had craggy features, strong jaw, eagle eyes under beetling brow, a man rough hewn and confident. I found him intimidating at first but with a wry twinkle in his eyes that sparkled as we talked. We talked for a good hour warming to each other's company. Then, recalling the time, I took my leave and patting Molly, this time with genuine tenderness, I left and walked back towards my cottage. It was dark long since, and as I strolled away, I was vaguely conscious of light flooding from the pub door behind me as, I imagined, other drinkers were leaving. I turned to see, but there was no-one. It was only as I turned the key in my door that I realised Molly was at my heels.

What was I to do? Gently I took her muzzle, indicated the pub along the road. 'Go, Molly, GO.' Do dogs understand directions? And I closed my front door, leaving her outside.

I was already in bed, my half-specs on and a manuscript on my knees when there was a thunderous banging on the door. It was no surprise to find Molly's owner there and now quite angry at what was happening, but unable to direct his anger at either me or his beloved Molly. He simply grunted his displeasure, then picked her up and carried her off to his car.

Does anything I have told you so far make sense? It didn't to me. I was bewildered. What could be attracting this lovely and devoted animal to an indifferent and preoccupied working woman. Next morning I decided on steps that I calculated would stop such a thing happening again. I bathed, using different soap and different scent. I dressed in different clothes, tied my long hair back in a ribbon, presented myself to the world as a changed person. When I went to the door to collect the daily paper, Molly was lying patiently across the threshold.

Oliver – this I knew by now was her owner's name – arrived in time for coffee midmorning. Something had changed in him. He wasn't cross any more, or even bewildered. 'If you're set on stealing my dog's affections,' he said 'you're going to have to take me on as well.' And the craggy smile gave me such a sense of gentleness and concern that I didn't demur.

So that is what happened. We became close almost instantly and were married three months later. I moved my fax machine into Oliver's rambling manor house and kept my romantic novelists in order from there. Oliver was far more involved with animals than I could ever be. His work dealt with the study of animal behaviour, conducted in a small extension of the local university set up in the village. So nothing animals do really surprises him. 'There's lots we don't yet understand, you know,' he says, patting Molly and giving me a knowing but mysterious smile.

And this is where I need your advice. You see, last week we drove the Land Rover, with Molly in the back, to a village some ten miles away to buy a garden bench from a local craftsman. On the way back we stopped at the village pub, The Crossed Keys, for a quiet drink. It was Friday night and the place was quite noisy with people starting the weekend in a spirit of celebration. It wasn't as congenial as our own Ring o' Bells, so Oliver touched my hand suggesting we go. But Molly was nowhere to be found. She's getting on a bit now and not as sprightly as when I first knew her. So we were surprised she'd gone off on her own. I followed Oliver round the bar in search of her. What I saw then, rather shocked and later worried me. She was sitting at the feet of a young women, a bright-eyed laughing girl with a head of tossing black curls who was joking with two young men playing darts. But it was Molly who made me stare. She had nuzzled her nose into the girl's lap and was gazing at her with a yearning and devotion that I slowly realised was familiar to me. I turned to

Oliver who was looking from Molly to the girl and back again. He didn't look at me, but left the pub in silence and sat waiting behind the wheel of the Range Rover until I joined him.

'She doesn't want to come with us,' I said slowly, and with apprehension. 'No,' he said, softly turning the key in the ignition and pulling away from The Crossed Keys. We haven't spoken of it since. Molly has not returned, and several days have passed without her. What can I do, do you think? I feel curiously threatened. I wish I understood animals better.

SIMON HOGGART

Citizen Coon

o ◯ o

The first racoon I ever met was in northern California, while I was on a camping trip with an English family. He came out of the woods one night and peered at us from what, misleadingly, seemed to be a safe distance. Like much North American fauna (chipmunks, blue jays and moose come to mind), racoons resemble cartoon characters more then real animals; they have furry Lone Ranger masks, so one can imagine them in little black hats, getting into comical fights with Sheriff Possum.

We threw half a chocolate biscuit towards him. There was no nonsense about waiting ten minutes before darting shyly towards it; instead he waddled speedily and purposefully forward, ate the biscuit, and sat, plonked there, waiting for more.

Next, by means of racoonish squeaks and squeals, no doubt already set to music by Judy Collins, he alerted his friends and kin. Cohorts of them strode out of the woods. The showed no fear at all, and simply marched, like the Grand Old Duke of York's troops, straight up onto the picnic table, where they set about eating our dinner.

There isn't an awful lot you can do about a concerted racoon raid. They are squat, bottom-heavy beasts, the size of fat corgis. American children are told they are probably rabid, so nobody wants to grab them and risk being bitten. In the end we got rid of them by throwing large stones – first at those still filing out of the woods, then at the crack SAS team which had originally scaled the table. It sounds dreadfully cruel but it was absolutely necessary. The boys in our party loved it. Flump! as a rock hit one amidships. Splat! as their mother's tomato salad sprayed into the bushes. We ate what we could of the remains while the racoons watched us beadily from the trees.

Years later, with a colleague, I climbed Mount St Helens in Washington State. This is a volcano, and at the time of our visit it was rumbling and shaking. If I had known that it would erupt eight days later, killing more than 60 people and sending up a ton of debris for every inhabitant of the planet, I would probably not have been there. As it was, we planned to visit Harry Truman (no relation) the curmudgeonly old man who famously lived near the summit, renting out holiday cottages and boats. He had refused to be evacuated. The following week he died instantly when the uppermost cubic mile of the mountain crashed on top of him.

We were trespassing on the volcano, which had been sealed off by the police, and worryingly our car had got stuck on a tree stump as we tried to drive round the road block. Worst of all, Harry Truman wasn't there. Just a row of empty cottages, a few boats on the still blue lake, and some strange scratching noises.

When we returned to our car, a state trooper had worked out what had happened and arranged for a truck to tow it off. He also explained we were under arrest. At that point, Harry Truman arrived, thrilled at the presence of more foreign reporters and desperate to be interviewed. I asked if he lived alone on the mountain.

'Nope,' he said, 'got maybe ten or a dozen coons up there for company.'

'Good lord, do you mean *black people*?' my colleague asked.

Truman threw back his head and roared. 'Aw no, not *niggers*!' he said, 'racoons!'

That's how people talked in the early part of the century in

Virginia, where he had been raised. Nevertheless I thought it wise not to include the exchange in my written account. (The trooper was also welcoming, and released us as soon as we were clear of the barriers.)

Years after that, my family and I stayed with friends in northern Mississippi, where their family owns a farm. It's probably the poorest part of the United States. Elvis's birthplace is nearby, and you can understand the hopeless excess of Graceland if you see the country he came from.

Our friend's father had caused some local ripples by appointing a black man his farm manager, but when you met Clark you knew why: he was dry, competent, laconic without being taciturn, and affable when moved to it. I felt that had he been a Highland ghillie a hundred years ago he might have won Queen Victoria's heart. One night Clark announced that he was going on a coon hunt, and we were welcome to join him.

Two huge coonhounds, Beagles of the Baskervilles, were locked into a wire cage in the back of the pick-up. We bumped along dirt roads until we came to a cotton field. It was early January, and cold; just a few bolls gleamed in the hard moonlight like the first sparse snowfall of winter.

Whenever we came to a tall tree, Clark would shine a powerful torch high into the branches. Finally he found what he was looking for. The eyes of a racoon gazed steadily back at him like tracer. He raised his rifle and shot twice. After what seemed an age there was a soft, then faster, whumping, thumping noise, like a teddy bear falling down a long steep staircase. The racoon landed at our feet and started snarling bitterly at the dogs.

But a trapped and wounded coon is no match for two big coonhounds. What followed wasn't attractive (I was glad our three-year-old wasn't there to watch) but at least it was quick. The coon, the first of three that night, disappeared into the vast poacher's pockets of Clark's coat.

Well, that's how the poor black people of the South eke out their living. The extra few dollars buys medicine, or the children's shoes, or just an occasional small luxury. The coon goes into the pot, and the pelt is sold. They used to get $12 or $15 each, but the anti-fur campaign has hit prices badly, and the price is nearer $7 these days, less than £5.

There's the liberal dilemma for you: well heeled *bien pensants* in New York gratify their consciences by not buying coonskin caps and so can save even more money for their $50 suppers, Donna Karan dresses and Virgin Island holidays. Clark's family are just a little worse off than they were.

ALISTAIR SAMPSON

Petty Points

o ◐ o

Tortology

When a torty . . .
          is first bought he
Finds it strange upon the lawn.
He pines for the sound of the pets around
The shop where he was born.
Now though he may feel shop-sick
This phase will quickly pass.
Just make some torty noises
And leave lettuce on the grass.

When a torty . . .
          is feeling sporty
He likes to have a race
With another sporty torty
At an in-excessive pace.
They feel it is no pleasure
To cover the ground too fast;

As sport is a form of leisure
The winner must come last.

When a torty . . .
                is feeling courty
He cherches a ma'moiselle,
Who can boil an oeuf and do soixante-neuf,
And is not just a pretty shell.
A torty that he can mate with
Who has no mother-in law.
A torty to hibernate with,
A torty who does not snore.

When a torty . . .
                is too naughty
He goes to a tortoise Hell.
He doesn't get his lettuce
And they take away his shell
For making little boxes
And now and then a comb,
Which makes a torty snorty
For his tortoise-shell is home.

Now a torty . . .
                may be a shorty
Who creeps along the ground,
But when the grasshopper hops it
He still will be around.
So what has the tortoise taught us?
This – if we wish to last:
Stay quietly put when it's cold afoot,
And never move too fast.

Paws For Thought

When a cat disappears for a couple of years,
Where do you think it goes?
Where does a feline make a beeline
For, do you suppose?
Do the Siamese scram to Vietnam,

And the Persians to Iran?
And where is it that a British cat
Goes? Is there a lonely barn,
Where wise old toms discuss atom bombs?
Or is there a long lost alley
Near Billingsgate where they congregate
For the annual pussy-cat rally?

Horns of a Dilemma

Dear Sir,
Would you, as soon as poss,
Collect your pet Rhinoceros?
Although I'm very fond of pets.
This one is rather large, and gets
A little in the way at times;
And as it's used to warmer climes
It's rather hard to see the fire,
And when we're ready to retire
It settles down outside the door –
You see, rhinoceroses snore –
So, could you come and take it back,
Before the bedroom ceilings crack?

P S. I quite forget to speak –
About the quads she had last week,
From which the first three (out of four)
Are very like the dog next door.
Now, though I'm not averse to pets –
I do not like Rhinocerettes.

Our Doberman

Our Doberman
Is a sober man,
He hardly touches a drop;
A little sherry at lunchtime
But he knows just when to stop.
When he has been for his walkies
He likes a glass of beer,

But he never touches Advocaat
Unless he's feeling queer.
He usually has his din-din
Just after six o'clock,
And clearly finds that Winalot
Goes very well with Hock.
Yes, our Doberman is a sober man
But do not give him brandy:
That last time that he touched it
He bit the postman's handy.

Aunt Ethel

Aunt Ethel keeps a crocodile,
A cobra and a bat,
For she lives in Hartley Whitney
In a rent-restricted flat.

She also keeps four eagles there,
Two bison and a linnet.
Her bedroom boasts a tiger-skin
Which has a tiger in it.

She's just acquired an elephant,
Two swordfish and a puma,
And a darling little python
With a splendid sense of humour.

Aunt Ethel's very strict with them;
She couldn't be constrictor.
Why do you think the landlord
Keeps trying to evict her?

JOHN WELLS

Monkeying Around

o O o

If you are in love with a monkey, never admit it. People are far too prone to jump to conclusions. The old joke about the two old colonels in colonial days discussing Carruthers can come very near to the bone.

'Pity about Carruthers.' 'Carruthers?' 'He's run off with an ape.' 'A *lady* ape?' 'Oh yes. Nothing queer about Carruthers.'

Looking back, I think I have probably been in love with monkeys of one variety or another for most of my grown-up life, and I have spent a good deal of time trying to justify it to myself.

I began by simply *liking* monkeys. As a child I had a little monkey glove-puppet with a pink cloth face, a smile sewn in black cotton, and bright brown glass eyes. You put your middle finger into a cardboard tube inside its head, and used your thumb and third finger to work its arms. It lost one of its eyes, and my mother replaced it with a blue bead that made it look very odd indeed, but I kept it long after the sawdust had begun to trickle out of the inside of its head and down the cardboard tube, and I think it's still somewhere at home even now.

When I was a young schoolmaster at Eton I used to hand out little plastic effigies of gorillas and chimpanzees bought in Woolworth's to the aristocracy and gentry as prizes for good work in French.

Then, in the Zoological Gardens in Madrid in the spring of 1964, I fell in love.

I was unhappy and I felt, as you do when you are unhappy, that I was going to be unhappy for the rest of my life. I was leaning on the wall of the monkey pit, watching the baboons knuckling about sniffing things, tails swaying in the air, or sitting legs akimbo, looking superior and staring into the far distance beyond the human visitors.

The baboon who immediately caught my eye was examining a peach stone. I was amazed by the monkey's powers of concentration. He frowned at it, tried it with his teeth, and then examined it again. He could have been a nuclear scientist working out how to crack the atom.

Then, very suddenly, he dropped the peach stone and scampered away like a mad thing. There was a lady baboon who had in some subliminal way attracted his attention, and he was now parting her fur with exactly the same kind of undivided attention he had been giving a moment or two before to the peach stone.

From then on I worshipped monkeys. They had, I rationalised, cracked the riddle of life. Don't brood on anything for more than a few seconds. The secret of happiness is a very short concentration span. It's not a creed I'd face a firing squad for nowadays, but it seemed convincing at the time.

I didn't really have a chance to come into close physical contact with monkeys until much later, when I played the part of the villain in the Hugh Hudson's Tarzan film *Greystoke*. All the grown-up monkeys were played by dancers in skins with computerised masks and arm extensions, but the baby monkeys were young chimps.

We were knee-deep in chimps, and I was naturally in my seventh heaven. The only disappointment was that they were amazingly uncuddly. They have no subcutaneous fat, harsh wiry hair, and muscles like elasticated steel hawsers.

We also had the world's leading chimpanzee expert, Dr Roger

Foutts, who had taught his chimpanzee Washoe to recognise a vocabulary of over a hundred words – if, for example, Roger said 'Book', Washoe would hold his hands together and pretend to read – and we spent long evenings by the sea in West Africa talking about Washoe and dolphins. We also had with us Rona Brown, the cheeriest and most sympathetic animal trainer I have ever met, who looked after the chimp actors.

When there were human tantrums on the set Roger Foutts would suck his pipe and say 'Typical primate behaviour', and Rona was full of tips for dealing with anything that walked on its hind legs.

When we got back to England her favourite chimp, Mandy, hated leaving the studio and would hide high up in the lighting grid. If you called her she paid no attention. Rona would shout 'Goodnight everybody', walk out of the door, and Mandy would come scrambling down in a twinkling, reaching out for Rona's hand to be taken home.

Neil Kinnock was leader of the Labour Party at the time and was always very reluctant to leave any social gathering. I suggested the trick to his wife Glenys.

The time on *Greystoke* led me in turn to propose a television programme to the BBC in which I would pretend to carry Roger Foutts's work one step further and teach a chimp to speak English. The chimp could then, I suggested, be persuaded to move its mouth about, I would dub over some dialogue, and the chimp could do a David Attenborough on the human race.

I went with the producer to visit some Brooke-Bond-type chimpanzees: they were full-grown and terrifying. The producer was a bit thin on top, and they embraced him like a long-lost uncle. Still hankering I suppose for Mandy, I insisted we use a younger actress.

Rona Brown turned up with Mandy in the studio in Bristol, warning me that we were going to have a bit of trouble with the lip movements, but I brushed that aside. We filmed Mandy sitting with me looking at textbooks, examining photographs, watching film in a viewing theatre, having a cup of tea in the canteen and she behaved like a star.

Then we began on the 'teaching scenes'. She continued to be

very amusing, disappearing under the table when I asked her to read the word 'Pterodactyl', and stretching her lips about in every possible direction.

After that we filmed her in the interviewer's chair. I had already recorded the interviews with various distinguished psychologists, and the idea was that Mandy would ask what looked like the beginning of the question and then be intercut nodding between the wise psychologists' and sociologists' answers. She did the nodding very well indeed.

I then struggled with one of the great masters of post-synchronised dialogue to make her speak. The nearest we got to human language of any kind, to suit Mandy's lip movements, was something like 'Phoooeywee-pup-pup-pup'. In the end I offered a voice that might just have emerged from her extended lips, and sounded faintly human. It did not sound female, so Mandy had a post-production sex-change, and became Max.

The producer, I think, blamed it all on my mad passion for that particular chimpanzee, and some of the critics were quite unkind, but no hint of public scandal attached to our relationship.

Then, years later, John Betjeman's granddaughter Imo, who ran a Me and My Favourite Animal column in one of the colour magazines, asked me if I could think of a good jokey one to finish the series. I suggested we should do a humorous piece about me living with a chimpanzee.

Rona Brown turned up again with a very nice chimp, a relative of Mandy's, who very obligingly posed for the cameras hoovering my office, polishing the furniture, lathering my face with a shaving brush and doing various other companionable things about the home. Bearing in mind that people will believe anything they read in the newspapers, I plastered it thick with the most obvious jokes.

I said the chimp would hide when I came home and jump out to give me a surprise. I said the chimp was always trying to embarrass me when I was on the telephone by dropping potatoes down the lavatory. I even suggested that the chimp's nocturnal howling on the balcony for its jungle home was sometimes taken by salacious neighbours to betoken sexual ecstasy.

That is now in the press-cuttings, and I have never yet

completed a serious interview since then without the interviewer turning off the tape-recorder, colouring slightly, looking round to see that the coast is clear, and asking 'How does your wife feel about your relationship with the chimpanzee?'

LESLIE THOMAS

Home is the Hunter

o ◯ o

You may not have heard, but the greatest dog in the world is dead.

He was mine; Furlong, a basset-hound of lofty eyebrows and low profile, stubborn, loving, funny, indolent and everywhere. There seems to be so much more room in this house today.

Nine years ago, when I first saw him, he was swimming like a log in the Berkshire Thames. It was the only energetic thing I ever witnessed him do. He was already a year old, the back-marker of the litter, brown, black and white with a posh name, Thamsmead Pegasus, the misnomer of the century.

I took him home and, with difficulty, stood him up in the garden. At once he descended to his belly, legs splayed, ears spread, body elongated. Those huge, bloody, misty eyes creaked up. He looked like a crashed bomber. I knew I was in love.

Furlong was a country dog, familiar with farmyards, a denizen of dungheaps. I see him now, ambling among dandelion clocks and thistles, his tail protruding from a cornfield, or furrowing in January snow, a painful experience for one of such shallow construction. (His brother Humphrey was at the British Embassy in Moscow where, so a member of the staff once told me, he spent many excruciating winters.)

My dog, from a line of hunters, was so pedestrian and vocal that he never caught anything but a slow mouse which he carelessly trod upon with one of his mallet paws. We have two other dogs, a Doberman and a hairy dachshund, both chasers. But rotund rabbits by the dozen nibbled each evening on our lawn, confident of the early warning of Furlong's baying. The rabbits will miss him too.

Few people approved of Furlong; everybody loved him, although most failed to realise it at the time. Those rug-sized ears, those shocked and sorrowful eyes, that body like a howitzer became known wherever those freckled and padded paws took him.

Oscar, the dachs, has lost not only a buddy but a bed, for every night he slept against Furlong's barrel chest, quietly gnawing through the basset's collar like one prisoner helping another to escape.

Jake, the Doberman, is puzzled. He must think that the old chap has gone for one of his extra-long walks. Tiger, the ancient tom cat, is missing a fellow pensioner and confidant.

Furlong was wonderful at sleeping. Deep, deep, he would go, descending into volatile dreams of being a great hunter, his legs going like pistons, strangled yelps coming from his throat. At other times he would shudder with snores. He could sleep anywhere, at any time. Once he climbed into the back of a van delivering carpets and awoke thirty miles away.

He would also eat anything, and the wrapping. He once trespassed on a picnic, devouring salmon, sugar and sandwiches, while the owners were picking buttercups, adding a final insult by cocking his leg against their teapot. He once accorded the same treatment to a toddler in a pushchair (who thought it was fun until it got the blame from its mother) and the sere boots of an old man who sat watching the world from the innocence of a park bench.

When I was the subject of *This Is Your Life,* my dog – my best friend – appeared only on film although he was present in the

studio. They said they feared he might be indiscreet on something electric and fuse the programme not to mention himself.
Later the producer admitted that he was excluded because they
thought he might steal the show. Might?

A born blunderer, Furlong was a familiar figure at the vets. He
had been assaulted by hornets, kicked by a donkey (whose infant
he apparently mistook for some sort of dog) bitten by both an
adder and a pony; this latter indignity being recorded by a television crew who were making a film at my home. Horse and dog
were supposed to be having a cosy confrontation when the pony
buried its teeth in Furlong's ear.

Once a veterinary surgeon told me that my dog was so ill that
he ought to be put down. My world shattered, I pleaded, and got,
some last-chance pills. Furlong made a startling recovery.
Joyfully I returned to the surgery only to find that the vet had
died.

At home, bereft and very sad, we've been talking about his
intransigence, his idleness, his many wanderings, his abject lack
of finesse. Sometimes when we have had a dinner party he has
sidled into the room and beneath the cover of table and talk has,
with silent system, let off relays of wind. Horrified, we would
watch our guests face each other with slow, astonished, unspoken, accusation.

For this he compensated by providing the after-dinner cabaret
which he readily enjoyed. Fixing his white-fisted paws at each
corner I would lift him to a crouch and command: 'Go, Action
Dog! Kill!' He would collapse with a great, bored sigh. He could
also perform a fixed grin, all fangs and gums, and, with some
help from me and his wrap-around ears, do credible imperson-
ations of a bank robber, a blind man, and a charlady in a head-
scarf, although personally I thought his impression of a dowager
duchess by far the best.

An American film producer once spent a weekend at my home.
We never signed a contract, but he rang later to ask if the dog was
available.

Furlong made people laugh. At his George Robey eyebrows,
his Queen Anne legs, his tail, white-tipped, like a candle, his
expressions ranging from downcast to lugubrious. Village

children would trail him mirthfully watching his undercart swing like the bells of Notre Dame. He did not mind. When they weren't looking he ate their Mars Bars.

Undoubtedly he was waxing old and clumsy. One icy night last winter I called him from his late trip to the garden. The lantern eyes shone in the dark. Then, stepping forgetfully forward, he plunged into our ornamental pool. Unerringly he swam, shivering, beneath the net that keeps away the herons, and in the end I had to wade in after him.

I shall miss him in the evenings when he clambered into my lap while I sat in my armchair, all fifty floppy pounds of him (some workmen weighed and measured him during their lunch hour, so I know). His smashed old face would close on mine, those hung, red, eyes would gaze and glaze. That's a pleasure I shall now have to forgo.

Years ago, on holiday in Devon, I entered him for his only show. It was a family dog show and he won two rosettes, one as best sporting breed (one judge referred to him as a beagle) and one (easily) as the prize tail-wagger. It was in a meadow by a river and after his triumph he paddled in the water. There are times when I think that was the happiest day of my life.

His tail won't wag again. He died after an operation and we brought him home in a shocking (I thought so) pink plastic bag which the veterinary surgery provided. We buried him in the garden beside a camellia which has thrived despite, or perhaps because of, his attentions over a long period. Afterwards I went into my greenhouse and cried my eyes out among the tomatoes.

Last night I lay thinking about him. Curiously, a tennis ball was being pushed about by the wind on our terrace. I heard it bounce down the stone steps. I knew it was not Furlong's ghost out there. He never chased a ball, or anything, in his life. He was under the camellia. Sleeping . . .

LOYD GROSSMAN

Subordinate Claws

o O o

In one of the most thoughtful books ever written about men and beasts, the historian Keith Thomas paraphrases the Elizabethan George Owen in praise of the lobster, an animal which 'provided men with food, for they could eat its flesh; with exercise, for they had first to crack its legs and claws; and with an object of contemplation, for they could study its marvellous suit of armour and thus admire the artistry of, in Owen's words 'the most admirable workman of the world'. I agree with Owen: God the workman certainly had his thinking cap on when he forged those delicious cousins *homarus gammarus* and *homarus americanus*.

Growing up on the East coast of America in a small New England town where lobster-fishing was a major industry and lobster-eating a year-round recreation, *homarus americanus* was the lobster of my childhood. I must confess that for me the lobster salad came before the lobster, and in order to find out a bit more about the life and loves of the beasts I decided to do my sixth grade science project on the lobster. So I prepared an elaborate chart featuring a full-colour cut-away view of a lobster and then attempted a plaster-of-paris model which sadly lacked charm, verisimilitude and whatever else you can think of.

Then inspiration chased away despair: I'd buy a real lobster and bring him into science class. After school the next day I bicycled down to State Street where most of the town's lobstermen landed their catch and bought a handsome chicken lobster. If you are not a lobster bore you should know that 'chicken' refers to size – one pound – not sex: this chicken was in fact a chap. He slept happily overnight in the fridge at home, resting on a bed of seaweed with a damp tea-towel thrown over his head.

The next morning we were off to school. In science class my lobster was star performer: noisily scuttling across the worktops, blithely knocking over bunsen burners and ferociously snapping his claws at the overly curious. Then it was time to go home, back to the seaweed bed in the fridge, under the tea-towel coverlet, to await his gastronomic fate. Would he be plain boiled, baked, stuffed, fried or fricasséed? Would he contribute to the excess of Lobster Thermidor, or merely end his days in a lobster pie? I opened the fridge door, rudely grabbed him by the back and raced down to the beach with him. I put him on the water's edge and watched him scamper into the surf. He never waved goodbye.

BEL MOONEY

Mrs Piggy –
a Short and Curly Tale

o O o

I first met Mandy Pinker when she came to the clinic, a note
from her doctor confirming the pregnancy. There are four of us
in the team, all experienced midwives, and I have to confess that
we aren't above the odd giggle at our patients' expense. Not that
we are suppose to call them 'patients'. Pregnant women aren't
sick, you see, although sometimes, when I see their husbands, I
think they must be sick in the head to let them anywhere near.
But then, I'm not married. All that stuff leaves me cold.

It fell to me to deal with Mandy, and I have to say that she was
one of the plainest women I have ever seen in my life. She was
very short and round, the shortness and roundness accelerating
by the minute, because of her condition. She had a plump face
(with the sort of cheeks you see on Christmas card cherubs) surrounded by a frizz of light, wispy curls. Her nose turned up at the
tip; balanced on it was a pair of large round glasses, with pinkish-grey frames. As she sat, talking dates, her small plump fingers twisted in her lap like a bunch of living sausages. That's
what I said to my colleague Anita, after Mandy had left. 'She

141

looks just like a pig!' I said, and Anita (who had seen her leave) couldn't stop laughing.

We go out into the community, or that's what they call driving for miles to see people who can't be bothered coming into clinic. So next I visited Mandy at home, since that's what she wanted. The place was almost impossible to find, but after many bad-tempered three-point turns in narrow lands, I arrived. The Pinkers lived in a mobile home about two hundred yards from the motorway, on a muddy plot surrounded by a small acreage given over wholly to pigs, pink and brown snouts down in concentration.

Mandy's husband opened the door, introducing himself as Reg Pinker. I thought immediately how uncannily alike they were, this couple. They say that couples who are made for each other look like each other; this must have been the best marriage in the county. The next thing I noticed, as Reg led me into the sitting room where Mandy was waiting, was that the small room was full – of pigs. A huge soft toy, about three feet high, bowed its head in the corner. Other fluffy pigs lolled at its feet. There were shelves full of china and plaster pigs: eating, skipping, lying on sides, back and front, with daisies behind their ears, cuddling each other – in fact doing all the things humans do. Except copulating, of course. There were postcards of pigs, pictures of pigs, an ashtray with a pig on it, and pink pig cushions. A scarlet piggy bank had pride of place on the table.

'Er . . . you like pigs?' I feebly remarked.

Reg jerked his thumb to the outside, where countless pigs snuffled in the sea of mud. 'They bring home the bacon,' he said, and we all laughed.

As soon as we sat down Mandy said, 'I want to ask you about sex, please.' They both went a rosier shade of pink, and glanced sidelong at each other. 'You see, Reg and me, well . . . we used to have it a lot . . . '

I opened my eyes wide, imagining the mobile home shaking, the pigs raising their heads, wondering what was going on, the sows' teats pouring milk in arousal, the boar snorting in his enclosure and lustfully pawing the ground . . .

Feeling slightly faint, I wrenched my mind back to what she was saying.

'Anyway, it's really uncomfortable now, because of this . . . (she patted her vast protuberance) and so what I want to know is, if it's safe to do it, you know . . . '

'Piggy-fashion . . . er, I mean, doggy-fashion,' I said.

They couldn't have noticed the unfortunate slip, because she nodded her head enthusiastically, and they both beamed at me.

'Yes, of course,' I said. 'As long as you're gentle, Reg.'

'Oh, I will be,' he said, and rested his hand on her thigh. I sensed they couldn't wait for me to leave, so I hurried my routine checks. The clatter of the foetus's heartbeat on my little machine filled the room, and Mandy squealed with excitement. Then I palpated the mountain of pink flesh – and that was it.

As I drove away I was aware of curtains being drawn in what must have been the bedroom. I smiled and shuddered at the same time. I do like my clients, please don't mistake me. But you see, midwives of all people have no protection from our animal nature.

Months passed and I got used to Mandy, Reg, and the piggery. I became quite fond of her, in fact, and her heart was set on me delivering the baby.

'If it's on time,' I said, easing the pink latex glove on to my hand to examine her, 'but if you're late I'll be on holiday.'

It turned out that she was late. When I got back from my church-crawl of Norfolk, the first thing I heard at the clinic was that Mandy Pinker had had her baby. It was a girl, and Anita had done the delivery.

'Perfectly normal – but phew, that baby took some pushing out. Ten pounds exactly. Proper little porker,' smiled Anita.

'Are they doing well?' I asked.

'You go and do the follow-up,' said Anita, 'She wants to see you.'

So I drove out to the piggeries again, on a bleak grey afternoon. The traffic whined along the motorway, the wind squealed around the corner of the mobile home, and the pigs seemed more numerous than ever. As I got out of my car one raised its head and gave a peculiar scream. It sounded almost triumphant. I picked my way through the mud, and rapped on the door.

Reg was please to see me. His face creased in a smile so wide his eyes almost disappeared in the folds of flesh. 'Come in,' he said, 'Mandy'll be that pleased! She's been dying to show you the little 'un.'

Mandy was sitting on the sofa amongst all the pig ornaments. The shelves were full of cards as well, for the birth, most of them pink for a girl. And cuddled tightly in Mandy's arms was a large baby, in a pink all-in-one suit.

'Look – isn't she beautiful,' whispered Mandy with reverent love, turning her child for me to see.

I stared. Above the baby's face, the mother raised her own to me, pink and fleshy with the nose more snoutlike than ever. I looked from it to the child, and sat down quickly. 'You're lovely, aren't you, my little kitten,' whispered Mandy, nuzzling her baby's ear.

'Little piglet,' I corrected, before I could stop myself.

But she didn't seem to have heard, or maybe I didn't speak about. For at that moment I think I started to have my break-down. *Piglet* it was. A piglet, so help me St Brigid, patron saint of all midwives. I saw the little eyes, and the pink bonnet with knitted ears, and the wide flaring nostrils of the snout, and the roundness of the pink dummy . . . *suck, suck, suck.*

I glanced out of the window to steady my nerves, and outside all the pigs seemed to be looking at the mobile home, closing in. Quickly I rose, stammering excuses about an appointment back at the clinic. As I backed away, Mandy's disappointed face bob-bing before my eyes like a pink balloon, I knocked a pig cushion to the floor and almost tripped over its softness.

'Well, don't go before Reg brings your present,' she said in a slightly sulky voice.

'Something to say thank you for all your visits,' he said, com-ing behind me and thrusting something into my hands. I looked down. It was a large plastic bag full of pink things. Blood smeared the sides of the bag; the fat was pearly white, the flesh rose pink.

'Nice pork chops,' grinned Reg. 'Wrap 'em separate and stick 'em in the freezer.'

I pushed them back at him, and stumbled out – calling over my shoulder, 'I don't eat meat, thanks!' You'll think me mean, but I never went back to see the Pinkers. Shortly afterwards I retired from midwifery, giving exhaustion as my reasons.

I suppose the trouble was that I've always been a little frightened of pigs.

FRANCES EDMONDS

The Bunny and Brush

o O o

It is doubtless a deprivation that has scarred me for life, but I never had a pony. As a child I begged for one every birthday and every Christmas until I fell in love with Georgie Best and started grovelling for a Manchester United season ticket instead. This, sad to relate, was similarly denied and I knew I would have to make do with Brush.

To others Brush might have seemed nothing but a thirty-bob besom, but to me he was a buddy. For years we shared a deep meaningful relationship – deeper and far more meaningful that most of the relationships which have subsequently claimed my attention. A sturdy chap of noble head, Brush spent most his time between the compost and the damson gin at the back of our garden shed. There was an indefinable quality about him. In his own quiet way, he seemed to radiate a purposeful solidity which, to a child of few mates and vivid imagination, was irresistibly attractive. In the right light, Brush could even look like Georgie Best but that was not his forte. For most of my childhood – if you did not count the brothers – Brush was the closest thing I had to an animal.

How would I have survived that pre-pubescent, pony-yearning period without his unstinting and unconditionally friendship? As I rode him around and around the garden, Brush would be my Black Beauty, my National Velvet and my 'Hey-Ho, Silver Away!' all rolled into one. All right – so he was never much good over the jumps but, with a rider high on Caramac and Cremola Foam, there was no stopping him on the flat.

Of course, a relationship so intense, so unsullied and naïve, was bound to end in tears. The genesis of the rift, innocuous enough you might think, was the annual school outing to the Cheshire Show. Now, in those days, the Cheshire Show was the high spot of mid-Cheshire's social calendar – a fact which speaks volumes for the variety of entertainment on offer in the mid-Cheshire of my youth. To put it bluntly, looking for action in mid-Cheshire was like an isometric exercise – a hell of a lot of strain and you got absolutely nowhere.

Every year the show would be teeming with rock-handed, ruddy-faced farmers all carrying huge wodges of spondoolicks and eyeing up the livestock. Gleaming in the sunlight, exhibitions of mowers, threshers and tractors attracted huge crowds of pint-pot toting locals. The blokes oooed and aahed, the way men do over machinery, and vowed that, come the European Agricultural Policy, they too would have several of everything Massey Ferguson had to offer.

There were beer tents, of course, heady with the smell of stale sweat and stout, and cake stalls and ice-cream vans and just about everything a young mid-Cheshire heart could desire. We schoolchildren arrived with our own packed lunches, lovingly prepared by our mums. Obnoxious pre-Thatcherites all, we soon had a free market operating in the sandwich stakes, with a going rate of two cheese-and-pickles for one John West tinned salmon. The market was distinctly bearish for boiled egg and salad. And, more precocious than the rest of us, Lydia Basset traded a swift snog behind the sheep dip for Richard Maxwell's can of shandy.

Generous as ever, the old man had given me ten shillings – riches beyond belief – with a general injunction not to pig out on pop. I can still remember the feeling of privilege and power that crinkly brown note conveyed. Roughly speaking, ten bob equated to one hundred and twenty sherbert saucers, thirty ninety-niners, or fifteen bottles of Tizer. Therein lay power indeed.

I was on my way to the sweet stall, weighing up the permutations, when suddenly I saw him. It was a veritable *coup de foudre*. The dark shiny hair, the cute retroussé nose, the liquid brown eyes – who would have ever imagine that a rabbit could possess such pulling power? The ten-bob note swiftly changed hands and Blackie the Bunny was mine.

The mater threw a wobbly when I brought the creature home, a reaction oft to be repeated as, partner-wise, I worked my way up the Darwinian scale of evolution. The rabbit, however, possessed a certain understated charm which eventually won her over. Relenting, she said I could keep him in the garden shed so long as he did not smell.

Oh, the cruelty and insensitivity of extreme youth! As I fussed over Blackie with tepid milk and fresh lettuce, never once did it occur to me that my old mate, Brush, might be jealous. I did not even notice when, distraught, he toppled over into the gin and his bristles fell into the compost. So besotted was I with Blackie that Brush was completely forgotten. Silly me! As observation of England cricket teams was later to reveal, even inanimate objects will eventually react. Betrayed and ignored, Brush was plotting his revenge.

It must have happened in the middle of the night. The next morning, as I danced down the garden to feed my new best friend, I noticed that the shed door was ajar. Trembling, I looked inside to find that Blackie, the beloved bunny, had scarpered without trace. The tears were coursing down my cheeks when suddenly I noticed Brush, horizontal across the doorstep. Quite clearly, the force of his fall had opened the door and rid him of his rival. Racked with remorse, I picked up Brush and gave him a little hug. Faithful friends are hard to find. I never asked for another pet.

BENNY GREEN

Greyhound in the Slips

o ◯ o

Although there was never any real money in my family, there was much talk about it. If dreams came true, my father and his brothers would have been millionaires a hundred times over. They were all convinced that the gateway to boundless wealth lay at the entrance to the nearest greyhound track or racecourse. I cannot remember a time when they were not adding the final touches to some infallible system, or following the devious trail of some intrigue to do with dogs and horses. My father and my Uncle Henry remain the only men I ever knew who perfected a foolproof scheme to cheat the bookies and still managed to come out losing. But that is another, totally ridiculous story.

   One of my earliest tribal recollections is of being taken by my father – my mother was at work, keeping us – to the local surgery because of my severe head cold. But instead of telling the doctor what the trouble was, my father opened the conversation with: 'Can you give me something to make a dog run faster?' to which the doctor, who was an even worse case than my father, replied, 'No, but I can give you something to make the other five run slower.' Only once in my life did any of this rub off on me, for I have never been much of a gambler. There was one escapade in the speculative past of my father's which will remain with me till they carry me out by the handles.

In telling the story of my relationship with Frisco Kelly, I am aware I may be breaching a few confidences, but the affair has been on my conscience for so long now that I think it best to give an account of myself and let history be the judge. Frisco Kelly was a dog I once knew, a racing greyhound with a personality all his own, and one, incidentally, which was a flat contradiction of his name. Who the noodle was who christened him I have no idea, but he certainly got it all wrong. Frisco Kelly. It sound like a cross between a wharf rat and a hat-check girl in a low night club. In fact Kelly was highly civilised with a fastidious pride and a sense of breeding sadly lacking in those who guided his fortunes. He could at least claim to know who his grandfather was, and there must have been many in the dog-racing world who envied him for that.

I think the best way of conveying his urbanity is to say that had the paw been on the other foot and he a human, he would have spurned the very idea of dog-racing as a footling waste of time. As for myself, I can at any rate claim that I still remember him, which is more than can be said for all those mindless multitudes so long ago who shouted and screamed at him to run faster and jeered and hooted him and cursed him from hock to hackle on those occasions, which occur in every dog's life, when he felt disinclined to bother.

Frisco Kelly came into my life one wartime morning when my father, whose grasp of the principles of a true renaissance education was as firm as any man's, suggested that I might best be furthering the pursuit of wisdom by playing truant and accompanying him on a little jaunt to the Stamford Bridge stadium. Well, the sun was shining that spring morning, and I knew we were due for a session of *The Aeneid* with our splendidly moustachioed Latin mistress, followed by an afternoon of jumping over bits of wood at the behest of a gym instructor whose intellectual processes were so foggy that he was still struggling to work out the implications of the Battle of Omdurman. When I thought of

150

all this, I saw that it had to be Stamford Bridge, a decision which would have been met with pursed lips at County Hall and the loud cheers of Dickens, Shaw, Twain, Runyon and all the other wise men who had somehow managed to rub along unencumbered by the impedimenta of academic diplomas.

We were to attend Stamford Bridge that morning to observe a ceremony known as the handslipping trials. I should explain that the term 'handslipping', unlike the cowardly bowdlerising evasions of *The Aeneid*, means exactly what it says, and defines the process by which a young greyhound, uninitiated into the primal joy of being caged in a trap and released on an electronic signal, is held by the collar and then given its freedom to do absolutely anything it likes provided it runs round the track as fast as it can. In this way the gentry can get some idea of its future usefulness as a device for getting hold of some ready money without going to work, an ambition, by the way, which has always seemed to me to be quite admirable. It must be realised that this whole process remains unsullied by the faintest tincture of sentimentality. It was, and is, a question purely of stopwatches and speculation, or even in dark times, of pedigree and peculation.

Now my Uncle Henry had lately fallen into the crazy habit of purchasing greyhounds of Irish extraction with a view to winning the Greyhound Derby. At any rate that was how he put it. I think what he must have meant was for the dog to win the Derby and he to collect the profits. The question of what to do with all the winnings seemed to be academic, for so far his investments had not been blessed with good fortune. The last pedigree pup but one before Frisco Kelly had fallen out of the taxi on arrival at the kennels, done something dire to one of its back legs and spent the rest of its life in cosseted retirement on a farm, its racing career having ended before it began. While this was good for the pooch it was bad for my uncle, who was beginning to despair of ever seeing a dog of his rise into racing history.

So there we huddled, high in the main stand of the stadium on that long-lost morning, watching six apprentice racers, Kelly among them, led to the line and then released by a man with a stopwatch, a white coat and a purple nose. What happened next is an interesting demonstration of how sometimes real life can turn out to be more educational than all the schoolbooks in the world. There was some bumping and squealing and scrambling, a vague hint of scampering feet, and then a brindled blur streaking round the track, taking the bends with a Euclidean eye for the shortest way home, and completing the lap some sixty yards ahead of its nearest rival.

The whole thing was over in less than thirty seconds, but while it was happening time seemed to elongate itself, so that I had infinite leisure to observe the reactions of the rest of the family. At first they clearly assumed there had been some mistake. My uncle kept peering down at his slip of paper, as though suspicious that someone else's animal had been substituted for his own. He racked his brains to remember what colour Frisco Kelly was. Surely it was a brindled two-year-old? This incredulity modulated swiftly into terror at the sheer beauty of the spectacle before him. I suppose it must have seemed to him like one of those events which happen only to other people, like winning the pools, or being left a fortune by a relation you never knew you had. Meanwhile my father sat next to me, frozen to the bench, his face displaying a deathly pallor. I learned more in those thirty seconds about the causal links between external events and facial expressions than all the professors in the world could have conveyed in a million years.

When it was over, everyone stood up and stared down at the track, where Frisco Kelly, having slaughtered the opposition, was keeping his own counsel as always, quietly cropping the long grass at the side of the track. Then everyone ran down to the fence, leaving me alone to ponder the wonder of those moments when everyday life suddenly decides to conform to those stories you used to find in the tuppeny bloods. I was glad I had come. I was more than glad. I, who even in my teens had been present at one of the historic moments in our saga, perhaps at the very watershed for the family fortunes. I had witnessed that apocalyptic moment when the greater world had at last opened its arms and beckoned us in. One day I would tell my grandchildren how the canine miracle worker, Frisco Kelly, had come among us, bringing gifts beyond the dreams of average.

Events moved fast after that. Kelly was immediately entered in the first race at a suburban track and won in a canter. (I should explain that there are eight races to each meeting, and that ability rises from the first race to the fifth, after which it falls away, till the last race matches the first in modesty of accomplishment.) After that Kelly was entered for another opening race, just in case there had been some mistake. But there had been none, and Kelly won looking over his shoulder. He was then raised to the eminence of the second race, which he won with his front legs wrapped behind his ears. So they put him into the third race, which he won with the handicapper tugging at his tail, by which time it was beginning to dawn on us all that something unusual had turned up. In the normal way of things everyone in the family should have been coining it by backing Kelly to win while there was still time to cash in on his obscurity by getting what Runyon used to call a nice shade of odds. But this had not happened, and the reason why it had not happened casts a revealing light on the nebulous workings of faith in the punter's mind.

It so happened that the last dog before Kelly in the family kennels had been a weird creature called Waldron Blazer, whose attitude to life was just as distinctive as his successor's. But where Kelly had a panache which reduced his rivals to rubble, there was a strange philosophic base to the Blazer's ruminations, embracing the tenet that it is better to compete than to win, an idea which expressed itself in the most uplifting way. The Blazer considered it ungentlemanly to overtake another dog, so that he would get up among the leaders and try to lick their noses. Perfectly content to finish second himself, he could never bear to impose this indignity on the other dogs, so that no matter how poor the field, it was always he who brought up the rear. At last they tried to get his dander up by giving him a live hare, hoping that the taste of blood would imbue him with the will to win. But blood never came into it with the Blazer, who playfully nudged the hare over and then gambolled round it like a spring lamb in a nursery rhyme. He was a pacifist and a humanist whose name, unlike Kelly's, was a perfect expression of his temperament. If it were possible for a dog to wear a blazer, he would have worn one; MCC colours, I shouldn't wonder. The upshot was that when Kelly arrived, it seemed too good to be true. His owner refused to believe it, and when at last Kelly was entered for the exalted fourth race on the Easter Monday at Stamford Bridge, the feeling was that the bubble was about to burst.

It was at this point that Kelly and I were formally introduced. For reasons, I forget, my uncle brought Kelly home from the kennels for a Sunday visit, which is how the racer and yours truly came to be strolling the back streets of Euston together. I must explain that although a robust adolescent, I had had no dealings with dogs in my life before, and was therefore not conversant with the speed at which they can adjust their whims. One moment Kelly was trotting along on the lead, docile as a lambkin, and the next he was flashing out of sight across the desert of Sunday morning. Panic-stricken, I ran around the street looking for him, and finally located him among the rubble of an ancient bomb crater in Howland Street, where he was rousting around looking for something to eat. Just as I reached him and snatched the lead, he was crunching the remains of a turkey carcass, vast and antique, as though it were an ice-cream cornet. I pulled him away, but the damage was done.

What to do? A racing greyhound is so delicate a creature that a cup of cold water can reduce him to an also-ran. Our doctor's words came back to me . . . 'No, but I can give you something to make the other five run slower.' It was clear that Kelly would win no races the next day. But how to confess? If I told my uncle he might never forgive me. If it didn't tell him, he might back Kelly to win in good faith. Should I tell my father? The same predicament. And yet how could I say nothing and watch Kelly go down to dyspeptic defeat with the family fortunes riding on him? I looked for guidance into Kelly's calm brown eyes. Nothing there. He was licking his chops and nuzzling the thigh of this benign lunatic who let him run loose and eat old bones. In my confusion I realised that in the moment of crunching that bone, Frisco Kelly and I became indissoluble. He had found somebody to love at last. It was a moral dilemma fit for a Russian novelist, and not being one myself, I am afraid I ducked the issue. I took Kelly back to my grandfather's house, handed him over to my uncle, said not a word, and hoped for the best.

If you have been wondering all this time why Frisco Kelly

154

never went on to win the Derby and end up stuffed as a prodigy in the Natural History Museum, the answer is that he wasn't quite the genius he seemed. Apparently when my uncle acquired him he was sold a pup in more ways than one. Kelly, so far from being a naïve two-year-old, was in fact a veteran three-year-old, which explains why he so nonchalantly annihilated the field that morning at Stamford Bridge.

After a year or so, my uncle sold Kelly, who went off to the provinces and won more than twenty races for his new owners; he was eventually retired and put out to stud because of a tendency to grumpiness which gradually emerged as he grew older. To this day I regret not being in a position to respond to his gesture of affection on that once-upon-a-time Sunday morning. I never saw him again after the incident of the turkey bones, for which reason in an odd sort of way he remains in my mind as alive and well now as he was on that Easter Monday afternoon, when he came from behind in the fourth race to win by a short head. Nobody in the family had a bean on him. They simply couldn't believe it was happening.

CLAIRE RAYNER

All Things Bright and, er . . .

o O o

It is hard to love a stick insect. It is not easy to feel fondness for crickets, Xenopus toads, axolotls, slow worms, earthworms and assorted frogs.

I, however, have had to learn to stretch the milk of human kindness to the nourishment of these lesser creatures, though how I dare call them lesser I am not sure; as you will see if you read on, there are strong family reasons why I should not speak slightingly of any part of the brute creation.

The reason for this is my older son. A child of bewitching aspect in his babyhood, with an air of sweet innocence that would shame a Della Robbia angel, this infant at the age of two tottered in from the garden with his new friend, a worm. Large, pink (a dusky purple around Adam's clutching hand, I must admit) and decidedly repellent. Its structure and shape gave it unpleasant Freudian overtones I did not care to think about. Adam declared his life-long adoration of this creature (he said its name was Edward) and insisted on sleeping with it.

The next day I found him trying to push Edward through a

minute hole in an air brick. When I said mildly that this was hardly the way to treat a friend, he told me indignantly that of course he was Edward's friend. Edward lived in the brick, had lost his front door key and Adam was helping him climb in through the window.

From then on, it was magic in our house. He seemed to have some sort of Doctor Dolittle ability to attract creatures, the uglier the better. Local children fetched him unusual insects they discovered, knowing of his passion. He fitted his room with ant hotels, the garden with hedgehogs, and begged/bullied/cajoled us into digging a pond for him for his massive collection of tadpoles from a local stream, on the understanding that he would get the balance 'right' (whatever that was) and it would never need cleaning at all. Amazingly he managed it (he was six by this time) and the pond hissed with activity. In spring it was the site of the most amazing sex orgy as the frogs this child had coaxed into his pond, using some sort of Pied Piper of Hamelin tricks, bonked themselves stupid in layers six deep and turned the dark water into a disgusting simulacrum of tapioca pudding, the sort that used to make me throw up when I was a child myself. His passion for these creatures was so deep and abiding that we, his despairing parents, came to the conclusion that his one aim in life was to meet a beautiful girl, kiss her, and have her turn into a frog.

The next stage involved creatures larger than insects. Although he was busy rearing a family of very noisy crickets in the boiler house, which escaped via a hole under the skirting board into my study and nearly drove me demented, and had a stick insect known as Modigliani (well, he lived in an artistic household) which liked nothing better than to wander about the house and find its way onto the platen of my typewriter where it would stand and sway on its long legs, daring me to move it, he 'needed' (the word was clear; it was a deep and desperate requirement without which Adam would have died) gerbils.

These too lived in my study (no space in his own room, full as it was with worms and ants and the vivarium where Lilith the slow worm resided), where they turned out to be a veritable protein factory. They bonked (what was it about my household that led to so much sexual activity? I can't imagine) gestated, laboured and parturated and immediately ate the babies and started all over again. Meanwhile, they also shredded any bit of paper that drifted within reach of their cage and used it for nesting material. Very aggravating when it was pages twenty-seven and -eight of my latest Great British Novel which I'd completely forgotten on account of I'd reached page three hundred and forty or so by then. Rewriting them was hell.

By this time – he was ten or eleven, I suppose – we had lost all control of the situation. We actually started providing him with creatures as Christmas presents. The Xenopus toads, called Ascheim and Zondek (after the two doctors who devised the first pregnancy test with the aid of some of their forebears) they were without doubt the most ugly, unlovable things I ever saw. Adam adored them with the passion that passeth all understanding, and I swear they came when he called. Much of Adam's spare time was occupied in digging up earthworms to feed A and Z (when he wasn't tying lumps of my best steak, filched from the fridge, onto string to be dangled in the pond to feed the tadpoles). I asked once how he reconciled his passion for worms with using then as toad fodder; his reply was a model of objective scientific interest.

'The toads like worms,' he said.

But I think that the creatures that shook my hitherto barely maintained equilibrium most were the axolotls. I coped with sex-mad gerbils, I did not blench at red-eyed rabbits, misogynistic geese (he had two of *them*), the most noisome of guinea pigs. I fed the cat willingly, I helped nurse birds with broken wings, I learned to live with finding assorted bits of dead creatures in bags in my freezer waiting till Adam had the time to stuff them. (We once gave him a book called *101 Things a Boy Can Do*; one of them was taxidermy and he became a keen preserver of his friends in their afterlife) but I drew the line at cannibalistic axolotls that didn't wait till their dinner was dead.

In other words, these two repellent salamanders ate each other from the tail upwards. One tail disappeared and then the other. Then they fed each other their hind legs. I kid you not. This is, apparently, or so Adam assured me serenely, what axolotls do best; they have no nervous systems to speak of and feel no pain but they do get hungry.

I fled from his room and never went in again (it was getting too damned crowded in there anyway). I never did find out what happened in the end. Did they finish up as just two pairs of snapping jaws? Possibly.

Anyway, all is now peace in our home. Adam has married and has his own pond. He visits us (or rather he visits the cat) and it's always a joy to see him. But I still wouldn't dream of putting my hands in his pockets. They always used to be full of maggots he was rearing to be bluebottles. God knows what's in them now.

George Melly

Cub Reporter

o O o

The holidays have started after a most hectic and diverse early July. I'm at the Tower, nerve-ends unravelling, taking in great gulps of sleep, the adrenalin level going down like the mercury in a thermometer after a fever. Even the weather, a gale this morning, thin rain this afternoon, seems like a benison.

Nevertheless, the Tower is haunted this late summer by a small, lithe spectre: sharp-nosed, amber-eyed, needle-toothed. Its name is James. In April, Beryl Fury, the formidable miner's wife whom we met last summer during the strike, offered Diana a fox-cub to look after. Its mother had been killed and Ms Fury, whose love of animals is equal to her dislike of Mrs T, was unable to take it on. Beside innumerable other creatures, she has a fox of her own who, although adult and wild, still pays her the odd sociable visit and wouldn't take kindly to a new pretender to her affections. So James arrived; a round, sweet-smelling bundle, bluish-brown and more kitten-like than foxy.

When I first heard, I was initially resistant. It seemed somehow very 'sixtyish' to have a fox, but once I'd seen it I was as besotted as everyone else. He was named 'James Fox', not after the actor, but in homage to the author of *White Mischief* who has often stayed with us. This has sometimes led to a certain linguistic confusion.

I didn't see as much of James as Diana and the children – an abnormally busy schedule curtailed my occasional visits to Wales – but he made several trips to London so I was very much aware of the rapid emergence of the wild creature from the helpless bundle; the black-tipped ears bigger, the muzzle longer, the tail, tipped with white, less stumpy. His movements, too; sudden leaps sideways, rapid withdrawal when startled, instant silent materialisations, a loping trot around and over the furniture, all evoked the wild wood rather than the living room. There was no way then that James could be confused with puppy or kitten, although in some respects he seemed poised between cat and dog. Strangely enough, though, from his earliest waddling days he was self-house-trained, almost meticulous in his use of the litter tray. Early on, he developed a suspicion of strange men but an instant trust of women. It took him some time to tolerate me, but he eventually proved his acceptance, when in London, by springing out from a cupboard in the basement, where he had established his 'earth' in a hole under the sink, and nipping me playfully on the ankle as I tottered to the bathroom for an early morning pee. Here, too, if I wasn't very sharp in closing the door, and he moved like lightning, he would take a rather embarrassing interest in this function, resting his front paws on the rim of the basin until I had finished.

His passion, here at least puppy-like, was for footwear. My pair of disreputable but much cherished slippers vanished into the hole under the sink, although oddly enough *one* of them was later returned more or less intact. This was his pattern, to destroy one; a detective examining our shoes would have reached the bizarre conclusion that we were a household of one-legged persons. He could be naughty but, as Diana pointed out, while making himself judiciously scarce after the event, he showed absolutely no guilt. Domestic pets are often tainted by our awareness of sin. Not so James. He pre-dated the fall of man.

As he grew bigger a dreadful decision began to loom. It is

possible to castrate a fox, thereby avoiding not only its powerful scent but also its primitive urges, and to bring it up as a pet. This was never in question, but to drive him off from the Tower would have been a death-sentence. Initially he would have been too trusting, his award to be shot or trapped, and besides there is a local hunt.

Diana's first attempt to find him a halfway house was a failure; a well-meaning, hippy animal-rights commune in Essex called 'Bright and Beautiful', whose notion of weaning James to the wild was to shut him in a dirty shed for a few weeks and then abruptly set him free. She left him overnight with grave misgivings and returned next day to hear him howling for her. She reclaimed him, but only after he had fled to the woods for several panic-stricken hours. It took him ages to regain his confidence and, on the way back to the Tower, he bit her companion, an unheard-of transgression until that moment.

Finally, she discovered some foresters with a practical love and knowledge of wild creatures and, sadly but gratefully, entrusted James into their hands. He has graduated there from a kennel-run, via a deer-enclosure, to the woods, taking her slipper with him. He returns, secretly, to remove food they leave out for him. It must be him; no totally wild fox would enter a wired-in, trap-like space. There is no hunt near by, no farmers. He has every chance of survival in those virgin woods.

He will gradually forget us all, even Diana; but we, and especially Diana, will never forget him. He is certainly the best documented fox in history. There are dozens of photographs of him at every stage: leaping, worrying objects, sleeping, strutting across the back of a sofa. My step-daughter Candy has celebrated him in a little book called *Red Mischief* in which these images are reinforced by suitable quotes from poets and writers. Meanwhile, we hope and believe James to be emulating Ted Hughes's 'Thought Fox':

> Across clearings, an eye,
> A widening deepening greenness,
> Brilliantly, concentratedly,
> Coming about its own business.

DICK VOSBURGH

Doggerel For a Pedigreed Chum

o O o

On 22 December, 1992, Rosie, the Vosburgh family's King Charles spaniel died, aged nine years.

December twenty-second. If you wait,
I'll list a few who died upon this date:
George El-i-ot, that novelist of rank,
Nathanael West, that novelist and bank,
Dwight Lyman Moody, ace evangelist,
Krafft-Ebing, pioneer psychiatrist,
And Harry Langdon, silent screen buffoon
Who found his own craft ebbing all too soon.
Von Sternberg's on the list, and what is more,
Aulus Vitellius, Roman emperor,
Upon this day was put to death in Rome.
And Rosie Kindrum Lilac died at home.

For some time she'd been dying by degrees.
And London's homeless now includes her fleas.
Although Vitellius fought with sword and shield,

163

I'll bet he never ran into a field,
Then realised he'd made a great mistake:
The field was *not* a field – it was a lake!
This happened to our Rose, who panicked not:
She taught herself to swim, there on the spot!
(We got more laughs from Rosie in a year
Than Landgon got in his entire career.)

Throughout her life, with pride we'd all maintain:
'Should any burglar enter our domain,
Then Rose will separate him from his breath,
By mercilessly licking him to death.'

But *famous* names today are our concern;
To Richard von Krafft-Ebing we return.
A noted sexual expert by repute –
But Rose got far more sexy with a boot.

Remarkably, when agitated, she
Could imitate a chatt'ring chimpanzee.
(That's more than you can say of Shep or Petra,
Old Yeller, Lassie, Rin Tin Tin, et cetera.)

A hundred years have passed, and still we read
George Eliot's *Middlemarch* and *Adam Bede*.
Eight novels reached the printed page, 'tis true –
But Rosie got it on the paper too.

King Charleses don't live long – she had to go.
She's up there, chasing cats around, I know,
With no more pills, no dashes to the vets.
So Happy Christmas, Rose, from us. Your pets.

Melvyn Bragg

Animals I Have Not Known

o ◯ o

Recently a young poet told a story about a dog. It summed up most of my personal experience with animals.

It was at the Brighton Festival. He was centre stage, facing a battery of microphones and a dangerously overcrowded above-pub room more accustomed to late night Grunging Rock. The number of microphones suggested a press conference. The audience was basically young, bright and undeviatingly attentive. This was the Word. These be contemporary poetry readings.

His parents, said the young poet, had recently been walking in the Peak District. One morning they had set out from their overnight B&B, on the next leg of the ramble. A dog followed them. They took no notice at first. They cleared the village and walked up the hill and looked down on the peaceful-seeming idyll in Derbyshire stone and were still a little amused, and I would guess flattered, that they continued to be dogged. Some gentle shooing did no good although the unaggressive mongrel managed to look, as they thought, a little ashamed of himself.

On they went to those unpolluted areas of northern England

which will quite soon make it the most civilised open-space retreat in Europe. Birds sang. Lungs opened up in relief. History was in the very hedgerows and so was the dog.

Mild shooing a mile or two on became firm instructions. These were rendered difficult through lack of name but the meaning was surely clear and the good-natured dog seemed to understand very well. He moved in apologetic semicircles, he bowed his cross-bred head low; but he did not make tracks back to his village.

On they went, the happy couple, a little less happy now in the beauty of the morning because of this responsibility. Here a blossom, there a bush, everywhere the sudden lurch into life of nature, and yet the free souls were constantly tugged back to a mundane reality by this damned dog always about ten respectful yards behind them. Walking along as if it did not belong to them. Trying to pretend it was just out for a stroll on its own. Hoping to see the prancing of new lambs perhaps and smell the new scents of a vigorous spring.

They tried twigs. They are English after all. Sticks were out of the question. But there were light winter twigs blown off the trees in recent winds and these they picked up and cast – taking care not to aim at the dog, of course – but in the general direction of the dog, because the idea of throwing sticks, or rather twigs, straight at an obstinate dog was one which in, the folklore attaching to such matters, had an odds-on chance of driving the dog away.

It failed to work. The twigs fell aimlessly wide of the sorrowful animal but he was no fool. When they tried their next trick, the clucking of tongues, trying to cosy up to him to get him to come to them (why? were they going to carry him back?) he made his excuses and stayed.

The rest of the walk to the next village was much more uneasy than it need have been even though they had resolved what to do. They would get a taxi, take the dog back to its mother village, find its owner and then motor back for lunch. Expensive, but somehow the only option and perhaps some good feeling would result from it all. They reached their destined village.

The dog slipped into a house about a third of the way down the only street.

He lived there.

Animals, in my admittedly unprofessional experience, do what they like.

I know that horses do what the gentlemen of Vienna tell them, and that seals leap for footballs, and that dogs deliver newspapers, and that elephants dance to Stravinsky, and I saw a cat circus in the South of France some years ago, very impressive too. But somehow I think it's all a pretence. Give them their real lives and they become impenetrable and completely unreliable.

I have had unreliable and rather searing experiences at different times in my life with a donkey, a goose, a ram, a goat, a white cow, a stallion, a bunch of young heifers, and a bull.

About three years ago I was at Lowther Horse Trials, the wonderful two-day event up in Cumberland in summer. Everything from the Duke of Edinburgh and his John Ford act with the stagecoach and horses, to naval cadets climbing up to heaven on wooden frames; and fishing experts, shooting, two tweed jackets for less than the price of one in a high street shop, the whole world of country sports on the rolling slopes of that ancient estate.

Someone whose name was rather like Sheik Abdul Hassain Ab Assad was most courteously introduced. He was as robed as Peter O'Toole in *Lawrence of Arabia* and the theme music brought the Arabian desert to the British North West; and he had hawks. Away he sent them and they swirled in the air like medieval missiles and back they came jingling and jangling in the wind to slap their talons onto his reinforced leather gauntlet. It was history. It was romance.

His prize hawk went up a tree and decided to sulk.

Three or four hours later, as the cars and the caravans straggled away, I passed Sheik Abdul Hassain Ab Assad (aka Albert Hodge from Wakefield) who was cluck-clucking for all his might at the foot of a great oak tree. Somewhere deep in its medieval leaf-spread high above, his hawk had found its own Sherwood and was sitting tight. Sometimes I think that Albert may still be there.

Cage Aux Folles

o O o

When the last hamster died I rang the local primary school and within the hour had removed thither every last trace – cages, towers, wheels, bags of feed – of its small and worried existence. Since then there hasn't been an animal in the house, unless you count the inhabitants of the wasps' nest under the eaves, and an occasional visit from the ex-husband.

That hamster had character. In the dead of night he would start up, whirring away on his wheel, chomping, scuttling up and down his tower, little eyes flashing. When the boys let him out for a run he would make straight for the lavatory and sit bolt upright, in what looked like eager conversational mode, in front of the bog brush. Perhaps it was love. Maybe up there in hamster heaven he has finally met the lady hamster with bristly black fur and a very long stiff white tail who seemed so resistant to his charms down here.

He came to us from an American family who had to go back to New York, leaving him behind along with several large spiky green plants and a flock of mourning boutique proprietors. His previous owners had been two girls, near enough in age to my boys to guarantee instant suspicion and prolonged hostilities.

These girls belonged to a charming chap whose ironic sense of humour belied his trade in public relations. He was a widower and I met him at the house of friends who thought we would get on. We did.

We went to the opera whenever his trade brought him free tickets. We liked the same sort of movies. We differed over whether to buy red wine in large or normal-sized bottles. Only when it came to gin did it occur to me he might have odd habits. He would never put more into a glass until it was quite empty and then he would measure it, precisely, if often.

One summer it seemed an awfully good idea if we all went on holiday together. Him with his two girls, me with my two boys and custody arranged back home for the hamster. So off we went to Spain where, under the diamond stars in their velvet sky, we held hands on the balcony of a pink marble mansion belonging, so we were told, to the manufacturer of fairly famous jeans.

I noticed, with a wisp of disquiet, that he had found a measure somewhere in the jeans magnate's kitchen and was doling out the *fundador* with a practised hand.

This, however, was the least of my worries. Downstairs his girls were screaming that my boys had thrown their clothes into the swimming pool and my boys were roaring that his girls had put itching powder on their pillows. I remember thinking, what kind of a man measures the *fundador* at a time like this?

It got better. We went to a vast complex of amusements based on water – chutes, slides, wave machines – and everyone had a good time. It got worse. Itching powder wars escalated.

We came home. The hamster didn't seem particularly pleased to see any of us. Perhaps the person we had boarded him with shared nocturnal habits that included wheel-running and tower-sliding. The girls filled his cage with tasty snacks. If there were Benettons for the hamsters they would have done him just as proud in the shirt and sweater line. The boys let him out and encouraged him to roam beyond the bathroom.

Anyone who has ever had a hamster will know what happened next. He vanished. Now I have had cats, dogs, fish and birds in my lifetime. There was even an orphan baby duck that the ex-husband brought back from the park one spring and kept in a folded-down sock.

Some of them developed mysterious habits, like the canary called Baldur the Beautiful, who would whistle only when my gran sat under the cage, or Bob the dog, who loved to swim far out into the filthy turbulence of the River Mersey. Most of them reached a peaceful end. None of them had the powers of instant invisibility this hamster possessed.

One moment he was there, making his exit from a cage crammed with small mammal gourmet treats. The next moment, he wasn't. The girls called and made *ch ch* noises. The boys made jam sandwiches and opened their comics. Out in the kitchen I reached for the duty-free gin and, pouring, looked up to see a small but distinct frown at my unmeasured hand directed from the adjacent male brow.

Hours later there was a funny noise in the sofa bed. There was the hamster, chewing the edge where the mattress folds into the back. It must have been delicious. Not even the removal of cushions and the delighted cries of onlookers disturbed his chomping. He was discovered at last in what looked like a state of ecstasy, tiny teeth sunk deep into the hairy stuff.

It was only a day or two afterwards that his former owners bade him a final farewell. Little did either side realise it at the time. They were to return, years later, after their father had married a fellow New Yorker. With sons, since you ask. It was at this point that my sons became their best friends in the world, and *vice versa*.

The girls arrived on the doorstop one night, escaping from what they seemed to regard as durance vile at some expensive summer school in Florence. The four of them sat long into the night, warmingly recalling the swimming pool and itching powder wars of long ago, opening out the sofa bed to see the last traces of their erstwhile mutual pet.

Their father, meanwhile, was with me in the kitchen where we were once more discussing his views on the baseball season and mine on Lancashire's fortunes on the cricket field. Not wanting to live too much in the past I overheated the blender, making

Bellinis from duty free brandy and a basket of overripe peaches. His bride was back home. She probably needed a week or two on her own to get the itching power out of her trousseau. But, just for moment, somewhere in the distance, I thought I heard a ghostly wheel whir.

MICHAEL PARKINSON

Mitchum Rides Again

o O o

Let met tell you about this creature I live with. He is black, slightly overweight, sleeps a lot and has just celebrated his 105th birthday. As I write, he concentrates on the important business of licking his paw.

I speak of our cat.

His name is Mitchum and for the past fifteen years he had been as much a part of our family as my sons, the mortgage, the in-laws, our dustbinmen and rising damp. He is a moggie born of a fleeting relationship between a pure-bred Burmese of impeccable manners and an alley cat. A touch of the Lady Chatterley's. The result of their liaison is a cat of stunning physical beauty and appalling manners.

Let me concentrate on the good side first. I could look at him all day. His coat is jet black and shines like the bonnet of a new car. Even though his whiskers are grey and he eats too much he still moves with an effortless grace and his eyes are like emeralds. What I like about cats is their contempt for the rest of the world, their inbred air of superiority. They are the most disdainful of creatures, much more beautiful and certainly more clever and manipulative than most humans of their acquaintance.

What about our cat's bad side? Where do I start?

The beginning is as good a place as any. He was only a very young cat when we realised we were harbouring a delinquent. Very early in his life he revealed anti-social tendencies that were disturbing in the extreme. Quite simply: he was a thief. The first indication was a stray sausage found on the mat outside the front door. When I came across it I didn't know whether to pick it up or call the bomb squad. It turned out to be a perfectly ordinary supermarket sausage, the sort born to be smothered in HP sauce or baked beans, but lacking in the pedigree to go solo.

I concentrate on the origins of the sausage only because it was important to ascertain its identity in order to discover what it was doing on my doorstep and who had placed it there. I am fastidious about sausages and I could tell it wasn't one of ours. It lacked that certain *je ne sais quoi* possessed by great bangers.

We were becoming immersed in this puzzle when round the corner of our house came the cat, lugging a large chop. This he deposited next to the sausage before departing. We were still debating this extraordinary event when he reappeared dragging along a piece of rump steak. Had we not locked him up immediately, the mat would soon have contained the entire mixed grill that the lady next door had been preparing for her husband's dinner. We didn't dare tell her what had happened. We just hoped she had an understanding husband, or alternatively, a well stocked freezer.

Fortunately for our neighbours the cat soon discovered a more bountiful supply of food, namely the wildlife of the River Thames. He did not have the easiest of debuts into his battle with other creatures who wanted to share his territory. In the first place he had difficulty identifying which wildlife he could handle and which to leave alone.

One day he saw a head bobbing up and down at the bottom of the garden and began his low and careful slither towards his victim, nose and belly to the floor, moving like a black snake. He reached the pampas grass on the river bank and then launched himself towards the victim. As he did so, he discovered that the head belonged to a large male swan who reared out of the water, spread his vast wings and gave his adversary a contemptuous stare. It must have been like coming face to face with the avenging angel. Mitchum streaked back into the house and hid under the table for two days. It was his first traumatic experience.

He soon learned and became a swift and efficient hunter. He made only one further mistake that I witnessed – when he jumped onto the back of a resting Canadian goose which reacted to this assault by racing down the lawn, wings beating prior to take-off. Fortunately our cat fell off half-way down the runway, otherwise he would have spent the rest of his life somewhere in the Arctic Circle. These were minor defeats in a hunting life that claimed mice, water rats, voles, squirrels and enough ducks to supply a Chinese restaurant for a lifetime.

Nowadays, he has more or less retired. Old age finds him relaxing on the lawn surveying the abundant wild life that today hops and chirrups around his recumbent body. Once they would have been dicing with death. Now the most they have to fear is a token flick with his paw or his amiable amble around a territory he once ruled. Not that his general behaviour has improved any.

What we did notice was that as the fauna increased, so the flora decreased. The pampas grass became stubble; healthy plants withered and died; young saplings became droopy before their time. Various experts were hired to give their opinion and suggested many causes from the destruction of the ozone layer to the Chernobyl disaster. The real cause was much nearer home. We were being deforested by what can most delicately be described as our cat's toilet habits. The problem is acute. How do you potty train a cat who is 105?

We have tried everything. But he seems immune to all the various powders and sprays you can purchase to deal with such a problem. One of our neighbours suggested pepper. He is now addicted to the stuff. We are now philosophical about things. We look after him and think it won't last much longer, one day soon he will head for the Great Cattery in the Sky.

Having said that, it must be reported that he shows no signs of bowing to the inevitable. He might have slowed down but he is certainly not withering away. If anything, he gets bigger and more solid. We are thinking of widening the cat flap. At present it would allow a bull terrier access; if we enlarge it we could have a Shetland pony as a pet.

Mind you, his increased girth has had a significant effect on our Christmas. In the past years he has taken a liking to the crib, mistaking it for a new cat basket. Up until this Christmas he made it his job to kidnap mother and child, visiting shepherds and their gifts, plus the Archangel Gabriel, so that he could make a new home for himself. One year he got stuck and a group of carol singers were amazed to witness a four-legged crib galloping over our lawn.

This Christmas the crib lay serene and unmolested. He's too fat to fit inside.

When I wrote about him in a national newspaper he became a celebrity. People sent him letters, one women composed a poem and when I wrote he was poorly after having had a run-in with a fox, a couple turned up at the house asking after his health. I think they expected to be shown into his bedroom where he would be on a saline drip with his paws folded over his chest. I must say he coped with it all very well. I don't think it went to his head.

I sometimes sit and look at him and think of life without him. I don't think we would bother to get another pet. For one thing it would mean altering the cat flap yet again and for another, for all that he is undeniably, cunning, devious, mischievous, stubborn, Machiavellian, guileful, tricky, two-faced, manipulative, exploitative, fat, greedy, flirtatious, fickle and exceedingly bloody-minded – he is also, quite simply, irreplaceable.

ROY HATTERSLEY

The Donkey

(with not the slightest apology to G K Chesterton)

o O o

No doubt it had a name. But we just called it The Donkey, as if it were the only one in the world and no more personal identification was necessary. Perhaps my father, a reticent man, thought that we did not know it well enough to allow ourselves the familiarity of Tom, Dick or however it was addressed by its close friends and intimate acquaintances. For all we ever saw of The Donkey was its lugubrious head framed in the top half of one of those ingenious stable doors which can be opened at the top and left closed at the bottom. So, although at the time I was untroubled by thoughts of sex and gender, I now realise that it might have been a Sally or a Sue. Calling it simply The Donkey probably preserved my innocence for a whole extra summer.

The Donkey was kept in a dilapidated hut on the edge of Wadsley Common – a finger of rocky, heather-covered moorland which pointed south into Sheffield and spread out in the north into the Derwent Valley and the Pennine foothills. The folklore – undoubtedly spread and probably invented by my mother – was that The Donkey had spent its working life walking in a circle in order to turn a wheel which provided the motive power for a grindstone. Certainly the cottages which hid the hut from the road had once been owned and occupied by self-employed cutlers. But there was a flaw in the argument that it had passed its days in brutal drudgery.

I was too young to question my mother's logic at the time, but looking back, I realise that if a brutal owner had really worked it until it could work no more, The Donkey would not have spent its declining years in the Wadsley Common Old Asses Twilight Home but would have ended up as a block of glue. It was my mother's habit to identify pets which has been ill treated and offer them shelter – often to the profound resentment of their doting owners. During much of my childhood I must have been at risk of being brought up with a donkey in the back garden.

The full relationship could not have lasted for much more than a year. But it now seems that I visited The Donkey on every morning of my impressionable youth. However brief our acquaintances, it certainly established in my mind a clear picture of all that donkeys are and should be. Had it been a severed head – mounted on the wall between a tiger and an antelope – it would have been no less revealing about the life and times of normal donkeys. But in my mind it came to represent the essence of donkeyness. Show me a bow-legged, floppy-eared, shaggy-coated, melancholy-faced little horse-like thing and I do not think of donkeys. I think of The Donkey.

My mother tells me that when – in 1938, at the age of four – I made my first visit to the seaside, I immediately assumed that the donkey which I saw tethered between the Bridlington promenade and the sea was The Donkey and that it had followed us from Wadsley Common in order to share a holiday. It was only when we saw a string of virtually identical animals making their sad way home in the evening that I accepted the possibility that my original acquaintance was not the only surviving member of the species. Even then, I insisted – correctly, in a zoological sort of way – that they were all part of the same family.

It was Wednesday before I could be persuaded to take a three-penny ride. I still have the equestrian portrait which my father took with the Box Brownie that came from the *News Chronicle* after he sent in the ten front pages and the postal order for 2s.6d. I cannot claim that I look at home in the saddle. All claim to horsemanship is undermined by the fact that I am holding the mane rather than the rein. But I certainly look better than the donkey. My father had not mastered the art of focus. So, although I was more or less my usual shape, the donkey was an equine tadpole with a huge head and tiny withers. It may be that picture that convinced me that riding anything, anywhere, at any time, is one of the world's least rewarding activities.

Although my father was not much of a photographer, he was an expert on short pieces of poetry with moral or religious themes. My earliest memories of Christmas are Gillie Potter broadcasting from Hoggsnorton and Thomas Hardy's confession that he would still like to believe that oxen kneel in their stalls at midnight on the eve of Christ's nativity. I am not sure if my father envied Hardy's early faith or persisted in the hope that the childish beliefs would turn out to be justified and that farmyard animals were still as pious as he once had been. But his general views on all these subjects meant that my visit to The Donkey were regularly followed by recitals of G K Chesterton's poem of the same name. My father read from either *Mount Helicon* or *Grass of Parnassus*, tattered school prizes 'for excellent work'.

I thought of The Donkey, with shout about its ears and palms before its feet, clip-clopping into Jerusalem for its 'one fierce hour and sweet' and I knew – even though I could not see that far down its back – that there was a cross on the tough, hairy skin to mark the place where Jesus had once sat. A couple of years ago, I spent a miserable wet weekend in a hotel in Provence, under the shadow of the great grey hills that Cézanne painted with such repetitive obsession. In the field beyond the drenched garden, the deserted swimming pool and the ornamental lake, a donkey was tethered to a steel pole. I went out in the pouring rain to see if much had changed. The cross is still there.

I am no better at geography than my father was at photography, but I think the Cevenne is too far away from Provence to allow any possibility that the donkey, which I saw in the field outside Aix was a descendant of Modestine, the ass that accompanied Robert Louis Stevenson on his travels. We 'did' Stevenson's account of that troubled journey during my third year in the Sheffield City Grammar School and I deeply resented the constant caricature of a nobly docile breed. Every time that Modestine dug in her heels or shook the luggage off her back, I knew that it was Robert Louis's fault, not hers. No other explanation was possible for a boy who had fed lettuce to the placid, disembodied head in the Wadsley Common hut doorway – and had been reared by hand on the principle that only his family really knew how to treat animals.

One of the popular records of my boyhood was Alan James singing the 'Donkey Serenade' from a Hollywood musical called *Firefly*. Scientifically, the words left much to be desired. For, in order to find a rhyme for fool, donkey and mule were regarded as interchangeable descriptions. But what worried us was less the anatomical shortcomings of the libretto as the ingenuity of the sound effects. From time to time, we could distinctly hear the cracking of a whip. When the noise came out of the old Marconi radio, we all shuddered. To this day, if my mother heard that somebody had kicked an ass, she would want to report him to the RSPCA.

For years, all my views on asses were influenced by memories of The Donkey. I was offended by Shakespeare constantly using the name of the species as a term of abuse: 'Call great Caesar ass.' (*Antony and Cleopatra*.) As I grew up from the booby traps set by the Sheriff of Nottingham for Friar Tuck, through the explosions at the beginning of *The Bridge of San Luis Rey* to the several assaults on the 'whisky priest' in *The Power and the Glory*, what worried me was not the death of the rider but the damage to the donkey that he rode. Hemingway (in *A Farewell to Arms* and *For Whom The Bell Tolls*) wrote almost as brutally about donkeys as he did about bulls. Rudyard Kipling was more of a mule man, but his Noah was particularly unpleasant about the asses that wanted to join the ark. But asses are related to mules, so I grieved at the stories of the ammunition boxes that they carried and the guns that they dragged across Africa.

But by far the most awful thing to be written about a donkey appears in John Steinbeck's *East of Eden*. In the local brothel in the Californian Sodom, an innocent ass does things which I

179

could not bring myself to describe. What is worse, it shows every sign of enjoying itself. The Donkey – my donkey – would never have behaved like that.

Mine was an intellectual ass. All head and, as far as I could see, neither heart nor body. He would have bowled cunning leg-breaks, not donkey-drops, and crossed Euclid's Pons Asinorum without one false step. Not for him the braying and the bucking and the kicking of his half-brother the mule. Every time that I saw him, I was told that he was gentle, wise and kind. Perhaps I was right to think of him as The Donkey, the only one of his sort in the world.

Douglas Adams

Maggie and Trudie

∘ ◯ ∘

I am not, I should say at once, in any formal relationship with a dog. I don't feed a dog, give it a bed, groom it, find kennels for it when I'm away, delouse it, or suddenly arrange for any of its internal organs to be removed when it displeases me. I do not, in short, *own* a dog.

On the other hand, I do have a kind of furtive, illicit relationship with a dog – or rather, two dogs. And in consequence I think I know a little of what it must be like to be a mistress.

The dogs do not live next door. They don't even live in the same . . . well, I was going to say street and tease it out a bit, but let's cut straight to the truth. They live in Santa Fe, New Mexico, which is a hell of a place for a dog, or indeed anyone else, to live. If you've never visited or spent time in Santa Fe, New Mexico, then let me say this: you're a complete idiot. I was myself a complete idiot till about a year ago, when a combination of circumstances which I can't be bothered to explain led me to borrow somebody's house way out in the desert just north of Santa Fe to write a screenplay in. To give you an idea of the sort of place that

Santa Fe is I could bang on about the desert and the altitude and the light and the silver- and turquoise-jewellery, but the best thing is just to mention a traffic sign on the freeway from Albuquerque. It says, in large letters 'GUSTY WINDS' and in smaller letters, 'may exist'.

I never met my neighbours. They lived half a mile away on top of the next sand ridge, but as soon as I started going out for my morning ~~run~~, ~~jog~~, gentle stroll I met their dogs, who were so instantly and deliriously pleased to see me that I wondered if they thought we'd met in a previous life (Shirley Maclaine lived nearby and they might have picked up all kinds of weird ideas from just being near her).

Their names were Maggie and Trudie. Trudie was an exceptionally silly-looking dog, a large, black French poodle who moved exactly as if she had been animated by Walt Disney: a kind of lollop which was emphasised by her large floppy ears at the front end and a short stubby tail with a bit of topiary-work on the end. Her coat consisted of a matting of tight black curls, which added to the general Disney effect by making it seem that she was completely devoid of naughty bits. The way in which she signified, every morning, that she was deliriously pleased to see me was to do a thing which I always thought was called 'prinking', but is in fact called 'stotting'. (I've only just discovered my error, and I'm going to have to replay whole sections of my life through my mind to see what confusions I may have caused or fallen foul of.) 'Stotting' is jumping upwards with all four legs simultaneously. My advice: do not die until you've seen a large black poodle stotting in the snow. It's something else, believe me.

The way in which Maggie would signify, every morning, that she was deliriously pleased to see me was to bite Trudie on the neck. This was also her way of signifying that she was deliriously excited at the prospect of going for a walk; it was her way of signifying that she was having a walk and really enjoying it; it was her way of signifying she wanted to be let into the house; it was her way of signifying she wanted to be let out of the house. Continuously and playfully biting Trudie on the neck was, in short, her way of life.

Maggie was a handsome dog. She was not a poodle, and in fact the sort of breed of dog she was was continuously on the tip of my tongue. I'm not very good with dog breeds, but Maggie was one of the real classic, obvious ones: a sleek, black-and-tan, vaguely retrieverish, sort of big beagle sort of thing. What are they called. Labradors? Spaniels? Elkhounds? Samoyeds? I asked my friend Michael, the film producer, once I felt I knew him well enough to admit that I couldn't quite put my finger on the sort of breed of dog Maggie was, despite the fact that it was so obvious.

'Maggie,' he said, in his slow, serious Texan drawl, 'is a mutt.'

So, every morning the three of us would set out; me, the large English writer, Trudie the poodle, and Maggie the mutt. I would ~~run~~, ~~jog~~, stroll along the wide dirt track that ran through the dry red dunes, Trudie would gambol friskily along, this way and that, ears flapping, and Maggie would bowl along cheerily biting her neck. Trudie was extraordinarily good natured and long suffering about this, but every now and then she would suddenly get monumentally fed up. At that moment she would execute a sudden mid-air about-turn, land squarely on her feet facing Maggie and give her an extremely pointed look, whereupon Maggie would suddenly sit and start gently gnawing her own rear right foot as if she was bored with Trudie anyway.

Then they'd start up again and go running and rolling and tumbling, chasing and biting, out through the dunes, through the scrubby grass and undergrowth, and then every now and then would suddenly, and inexplicably, come to a halt as if they had both, simultaneously, run out of moves. They would then stare into the middle distance in embarrassment for a bit before starting up again.

So what part did I play in all this? Well, none really. They completely ignored me for the whole twenty or thirty minutes. Which was perfectly fine, of course. I didn't mind, but it did puzzle me. Because early every morning they would come yelping and scratching around the doors and windows of my house until I got up and took them for their walk. If anything disturbed the daily ritual, like I had to drive into town, or have a meeting, or fly to England or something they would get thoroughly miserable and

183

simply *not know what to do*. Despite the fact that they would always completely ignore me whenever we went on our walks together, they couldn't just go and have a walk without me. This revealed a profoundly philosophical bent in these dogs which were not mine, because they had worked out that I had to be there in order for them to be able to ignore me properly. You can't ignore someone who isn't there, because that's not what 'ignore' means.

Further depths to their thinking were revealed when Michael's girlfriend Victoria told me that once, when coming to visit me, she had tried to throw a ball for Maggie and Trudie to chase. The dogs had sat and watched stony-faced as the ball climbed up into the sky, dropped and at last dribbled along the ground to a halt. She said that the message she was picking up from them was 'We don't do that. We hang out with writers.'

Which was true. They hung out with me all day, every day. But, exactly like writers, dogs who hang out with writers don't like the actual writing bit. So they would moon around at my feet all day and keep nudging my elbow out of the way while I was typing so that they could rest their chins on my lap and gaze mournfully up to me in the hope that I would see reason and go for a walk so that they could ignore me properly.

And then in the evening they would trot off to their real home to be fed, watered and put to bed for the night. Which seemed to me like a fine arrangement, because I got all the pleasure of their company, which was considerable, without having any responsibility for them. And it continued to be a fine arrangement up till the day when Maggie turned up bright and early in the morning ready and eager to ignore me – on her own. No Trudie. Trudie was not with her. I was stunned. I didn't know what had happened to Trudie and had no way of finding out, because she wasn't mine. Had she been run over by a truck? Was she lying somewhere, bleeding by the roadside? Maggie seemed restless and worried. She would know where Trudie was, I thought, and what had happened to her. I'd better follow her, like Lassie. I put on my walking shoes and hurried out. We walked for miles, roaming around the desert looking for Trudie, following the most circuitous route. Eventually I realised that Maggie wasn't looking

for Trudie at all, she was just ignoring me – a strategy which I was complicating by trying to follow her the whole time rather than just pursuing my normal morning walk route. So eventually I returned to the house, and Maggie sat at my feet and moped. There was nothing I could do, no one I could phone about it, because Trudie didn't belong to me. All I could do, like a mistress, was sit and worry in silence. I was off my food. After Maggie sloped off home that night I slept badly.

And in the morning they were back. Both of them. Only, something terrible had happened. Trudie had been to the groomers. Most of her coat had been cropped down to about 2mm, with a few topiary tufts on her head, ears and tail. I was outraged. She looked preposterous. We went out for a walk, and I was embarrassed, frankly. She wouldn't have looked like that if she was my dog.

A few days later I had to go back to England. I tried to explain this to them, to prepare them for it, but they were in denial. On the morning I left they saw me putting my cases in the back of the 4wd, and kept their distance, becoming tremendously interested in another dog instead. Really ignored me. I flew home, feeling odd about it.

Six weeks later I came back to work on a second draft. I couldn't just call round and get the dogs. I had to walk around in the back yard looking terribly obvious and making all sorts of high-pitched noises such as dogs are wont to notice. Suddenly they got the message and raced across the snow-covered desert to see me (this was mid-January now). Once they had arrived they continually hurled themselves at the walls in excitement, but then there wasn't much else we could do but go out for a brisk, healthy Ignore in the snow. Trudie stotted, Maggie bit her on the neck and so we went on. And three weeks later I left again. I'll be back again to see them sometime this year, but I realise that I'm the Other Human. Sooner or later I'm going to have to commit to a dog of my own.

· PETS ·
by W. RUSHTON

My current PET, this suave GELADA, who answers to the name of KLAUS,
Will stub his cigarettes out on my pillow.
But I've kept Bison, Wart-hogs (briefly), herds of Tapir, Cat & Mouse,
(Once you could not take a bath for Armadillo).
And I'd sooner have those CREATURES run amok about the House
Than LOYD GROSSMAN (or Miguel PORTILLO).